J. R. Worsley Talking About Acupuncture In New York

First published in Great Britain in 1982
Second Impression 1984
Third Impression 1986
Fourth Impression 1991
Fifth Impression 2004

Published by Worsley Inc.
Church Hill Farm, England
Printed by Health Communications, Inc
3201 SW 15 Street, Deerfield Beach, FL 33442, USA

British Library Cataloguing-in-Publication Data
A catalogue record for this book is available from the British Library
ISBN 0-9545939-1-X

J.R. Worsley photo courtesy of Stephen "Tuna" Flores
Cover photograph by Rebecca Chalker ©2004

Professor J.R. Worsley

D.Ac.(China), M.Ac.(China), N.D.(UK), Professor (China)

His Achievements and Honours Include:

- Professor of the College of Chinese Medicine, China
- Master and Doctor of Acupuncture, China
- Honorary Professor of the Department of Oriental Medicine at Won Kwang University, Korea
- Vice-President of the World Academic Society for Acupuncture
- Founder President of the College of Traditional Acupuncture, UK
- Founder President of the Traditional Acupuncture Institute, USA
- Founder President of the Norwegian School of Traditional Acupuncture
- Founder President of the Traditional Acupuncture Society, UK
- Professor of the Medical Acupuncture Society, South Africa
- Honorary President, Compagnonnage d'Acupuncture Traditionelle, France
- Professor of the Argentine Medical Acupuncture Society
- Founder President of the Worsley Institute of Classical Acupuncture, USA
- Founder of the Master Apprentice Program (MAP™)

Other Works by J.R. Worsley

- *Is Acupuncture for You?*
- *The Meridians of Ch'i Energy: Point Reference Guide*
- *The Law of Five Elements* (Wall Chart)
- *The Meridians of Qi Energy* (Wall Charts)
- *Traditional Acupuncture Volume I: Meridians and Points*
- *Traditional Acupuncture Volume II: Traditional Diagnosis*
- *Classical Five-Element Acupuncture™ Volume III: The Five Elements and the Officials*
- *Classical Five-Element Acupuncture Volume I: The Meridians and Points*
- *The Spirit of the Points**
- *A Library of the Teachings and Consultation Work of J.R. and J.B. Worsley* (DVD's)
- *An Introduction to Classical Five-Element Acupuncture™: A Public Talk in Seattle* (Video)

* Professor Worsley completed his work on *The Spirit of the Points* shortly before he died. Publication is planned for 2005

For further information about J.R. Worsley's work and where to study, please visit: www.worsleyacupuncture.com and www.worsleyinstitute.org

Dedication

This fifth edition of **J.R. Worsley Talking About Acupuncture in New York** is dedicated to Professor J.R. Worsley.

Without J.R.'s passion, determination and genius, this ancient healing system he once called "traditional" acupuncture would not be available in the West.

In the mid 1980's, a team of visiting professors from Mainland China visited J.R.'s college in Leamington Spa, England. After spending some time with him and the faculty, they concluded that J.R.'s teaching was a much revered and ancient form of healing, and "classical" would be a more fitting title than the more modern "traditional" label, hence the shift, *in title only*, from "traditional" to "classical".

J.R. created the Master Apprentice Program (MAP™) with the earnest wish that this treasured lineage would be passed on to capable and willing hands, hearts, minds and souls. Until days before he died, on the 2nd of June 2003, J.R. poured his energy into teaching and leading practitioners who had a genuine desire to learn this system of healing. He was preparing, with diligence and passion for excellence, as a Master would do, for the day he transformed from his earthly life.

I, as J.R.'s partner, wife, friend and student, love him with all my heart and soul. I pledge, as his Master Designate, to teach and lead this lineage as J.R. and his teachers would wish.

It is with abiding love, devotion and respect that this book is dedicated to the memory of Professor J.R. Worsley.

Judy Becker Worsley
(J.R.'s "Jude")

In Memoriam

Professor "J.R." Worsley

September 14,1923 - June 2, 2002

"For God's sake, laugh !
Love each other !
The greatest gift is to be loved,
And to love someone else."

Contents

Afternoon

After Tea

Questions

Praise

Acknowledgments

This is J.R.'s work and it is my honor to publish these delightfully informative lectures that he presented with such simplicity, humor, and clarity. I know J.R. would want to be included in thanking those who helped make this edition possible, so I am speaking for both of us when I extend *our heartfelt and grateful thanks to:*

Suzanne Burnell, who worked with me on this edition and whose attention to detail and enduring and kind support, personally and professionally, make her a much-appreciated treasure.

Sandy Dolan, Account Manager with HCI Publishing, who gave essential technical and professional guidance and steadying, diligent supervision with enormous integrity, patience and understanding.

Maureen Postins, who, working with extraordinary skill and dedication, contributes incredible wisdom and administrative genius.

Hilary Skellon, J.R.'s adored daughter, and our treasured friend and colleague, has blessed us with extraordinary kindness and support.

Meriel Darby and Julia Measures, dear friends and colleagues, who provide wisdom, comfort, fun and soul-level companionship.

Dianne Connelly and Mary Ellen Klee for their exceptionally generous support and love.

David Goodell, President of the Worsley Institute of Classical Five-Element Acupuncture, Neil Gumenick, Founder and Director of the Institute of Classical Five-Element Acupuncture Inc., and April Hulvershorn, who worked above and beyond the call of duty within the Five-Element Acupuncture community in a selfless and "high road" manner.

Charles Burnell for his generous editorial and administrative assistance and Max Alexander for his diligent and very much appreciated editorial suggestions.

Our family, colleagues and friends who provide loving kindness and practical help in ways far too numerous to detail. I am grateful to all who helped with J.R.'s USA Service (special thanks to Cecille Gumenick and Mary Ellen Klee) and UK Memorial Service (special thanks to David Shephard and Deborah Price of Performance Partnership, UK), and to those who helped create a Tribute Film (special thanks to Michael Munroe of Munroe Multimedia, USA).

The participants of the Master Apprentice Program (MAP™) who help keep the wheels of our acupuncture lineage turning with grace and integrity.

JB Worsley

Foreword

Following pressing demands from New York patients, friends, graduates and students of Professor Worsley's, I, along with other members of the Arica School, invited him to New York to hold a one-day seminar. He graciously accepted our invitation and on January 20th 1980, introduced by Oscar Ichazo, founder of the Arica School, gave a seminar to its members and the public on the subject of traditional acupuncture.

Having heard of him as one of the foremost teachers in the world of the genuine tradition of this system of medicine, I went to England several years ago to begin training with him at the College of Traditional Acupuncture in Warwickshire. Over those years I came to know him as a true master of this ancient art and science of healing and wisdom, as well as a teacher and mentor of great personal spirit, enthusiasm, humour and compassion.

All these qualities were evident to those who had the privilege of being present at the seminar. Fortunately we recorded the whole presentation and, such was the demand for a record of what J.R. Worsley had said, it was clear that we should not only reproduce the tape but make a written transcript which could be published. This book hopefully captures, word-for-word, something of the spirit and wisdom he shared with us.

As one who was present, and involved in organizing the event, it is impossible to describe all that we felt that day. We laughed, we learned, we realized so much - and felt full of gratitude for having the opportunity to listen to this man who is so self-effacing about his great gifts and yet so passionate that we should retrieve the natural art of being at one with Nature, and with everyone and everything around us.

Richard Apollo, M.D.

Preface

In the twenty or so years since this book was first published, I have been talking about acupuncture in many other cities and in many other countries throughout the world. It has been a joy to me to see the increasing acceptance and use of acupuncture in the West and most pleasing to see how discerning the general public has become about the type of acupuncture treatment it receives.

This reprint of the book has no need of updating, apart from some changes of terminology. The essence of the ancient wisdom is as clear as ever, as witnessed by the many millions of patients and the many thousands of practitioners each year who experience first-hand this magnificent form of natural healing.

I hope those of you who are new to the book will enjoy reading it as much as I enjoy talking about acupuncture. For those of you reading it for a second or more time, I hope it will serve as a reminder to us all that Nature knows best and we will do well to listen to her signals and assist her, through this beautiful system of medicine, to do the healing.

Professor J. R. Worsley

Morning

It is very kind of you to have invited me along for a beautiful meal last night. We had roast lamb, English style, and towards the end of the evening Oscar said, 'Now, what are you going to do tomorrow?'

Well, normally I just wait until I get to wherever I am going and 'do my thing.' Do you like the American 'Do my thing'? So, then I looked sort of frowning, thinking, 'Hey, we have things structured here.' He said, 'There's going to be an awful lot of Aricans.'

And I said, 'Well, who are they? People from space?'

And Oscar said, 'No, they're the cream of American intelligentsia.' Then he added, 'Of course, also there will be some patients, and they're even more intelligent.'

Then I started to get frightened; and then I started to go white and shaking. So I left his dinner and I went home to the hotel and I put a call through to the White House and I asked for the script writer to your President; and he was too busy. They put me on to N.B.C. News and I asked for the script writer there; and they were queuing up for this football match you have got on this evening; and in the end he referred me to someone else; and they referred me to someone else. And in the end I got to some pokey little house somewhere or other. I knocked on the door and a little kid came. I said, 'Is your Daddy in?' And he said, 'No, he's out.' I said, 'Well look, I have got to have a script for tomorrow.' He said, 'Well, leave it to me.'

And so he came round this morning, and he brought me this script . . . and it was very cheap. I can see why. And it has got written here . . . (Professor Worsley unfurls a roll of toilet paper) . . . 'Please read—this—very—slowly—because—I—can't write—very fast.' I give up!

So I thought I would start off by telling you about the three bears. Baby bear came downstairs and said, 'Who's been eating my porridge?' And Daddy bear came downstairs and said, 'Who's been eating my porridge?' Mummy bear came downstairs and said, 'What the hell's all the fuss about? I haven't made the porridge yet!'

I like this—at this time of day I like to hear a bit of laughter. We will get around to acupuncture; we have a lot of time.

After I had met the script writer, I was going back to the hotel and I saw a little placard saying, 'You know, if you want to have a real good night out, go round to this address.'

I was so worried about this script business, I thought, well, I would just go round to this address and have an American night out, as it were. So I knocked on the door, and a chap came to meet me, and he hadn't got any clothes on. Well, I thought, there's no turning back now, Jack; come on, have yourself a good night. The chap blindfolded me and said, 'Take your clothes off.' And I thought, 'My God!'

I thought, 'Well, anything for a good night out.' So I took my clothes off; and then after standing there about five minutes and getting really cold I thought, 'Well, to hell with this', and I took the blindfold off and my clothes had gone. I thought, 'My goodness, what am I going to do now?'

Then another knock came at the door and this chap came in and said, 'Is this where it all happens?' I said, 'Yes.' So I blindfolded him and said, 'Take your clothes off.'

Do you like his suit I am wearing?

It's nice to hear you laugh. That's beautiful; that's lovely!

Anyhow, we have come here today, basically, for two things. One is, I hope we are going to have a little bit of understanding about traditional Chinese medicine. I also hope we are going to learn a lot about ourselves. If we can go home just that little bit richer than we were when we came this morning, then I shall consider today to be really, really well worthwhile.

The one thing I want to impress upon you first of all is that there are many different types of acupuncture. And one that is predominantly practised in the Western world is what we call 'barefoot doctor', or 'local doctor'.

This is where we can put a needle in various parts of the body and we can take away pain. This is true. There is hardly any pain that we cannot take away by inserting a needle. But, of course, what happens is that after a period of time the pain returns. So what we are really doing is giving symptomatic relief. Rather like if you get a headache, you take aspirin and the headache goes away. But if there is a deep underlying cause, the headache will come back again.

Now, in China, there is a great need for local doctors, because the patient may be five, six, seven hundred miles away from the nearest physician; or as many miles away from the nearest hospital. So, in the little communities, they have barefoot doctors who more or less administer first aid. They take the pain away until such time as the patient can be seen by a traditional doctor, or can be taken to a hospital.

To learn how to become a local doctor is just child's play. One can do it in perhaps a couple or three weeks. And many Americans and English people have been going over to China, staying a couple of weeks, and coming back and saying, 'Well, I can do acupuncture.' They start doing this barefoot doctor acupuncture, relieving pain temporarily.

Then the pain returns again, and many of the patients say, 'Well, if this is acupuncture, then I don't want anything to do with it.'

It's a great pity, because we are getting many first-rate American and English physicians whom we need—need badly—who are trained in that method to become tenth-rate first-aid people. Local doctor is just like ordinary first-aid. It is a shame that many people feel that this is what acupuncture is.

Then we get the other type of acupuncture which we use for anaesthesia. This is where we can anaesthetize any part of your body so that the surgeon can carry out any form of operation without you having to take drugs of any description. And you are fully conscious whilst the surgery is going on. You don't feel pain at all. And many people think this is a kind of witchcraft or hypnosis. It isn't. It can be done; I have done it myself; and nine people out of every ten will lend themselves to this form of anaesthesia.

It isn't suggestion of the mind. We also do it on animals, so you can show it's not just suggestion.

This picture shows you a Chinese chappie undergoing major abdominal surgery, and you will see that he is fully conscious. He is talking to the surgeons about who is going to win the game this evening. You can see he is actually smiling and he has got half of his stomach lying out on the table. There is a lot of blood, and all that sort of thing. See, there's a chappie here just twirling a little needle in his ear. And there is another down the bottom twirling a couple of needles in his toe.

This application is valuable in one respect. It does prove that these needles are certainly doing something—if someone can go through that form of surgery and still converse with the doctor and not feel any pain at all.

And you may have seen lots of photographs where someone is going through major surgery and eating an orange. Why they couldn't wait until the operation was over I have no idea; but it is all drama. And, of course, this is the sort of thing that looks good on television; it looks good in the newspapers; and it is all in a way a sort of gimmickry because, again, it has no resemblance to traditional acupuncture.

I don't really see any of you in the room wanting to go through what that little chap is going through. I think I would rather be put to sleep and then wake up when it's all over. I am sure, if I do feel the need to talk to someone, I don't want to have surgery like that so I can talk to the surgeon. I would rather talk to him after, or before. And the thought of going through that frightens the life out of me; I don't know what it does to you!

Then the other thing we have to bear in mind is that in about three cases in every ten, the anaesthesia will wear off. You can imagine being in the situation that that fellow is in when the anaesthetic wears off. You suddenly become conscious of all the pain and discomfort. The Chinese are conscious of this too, and they switch over to Western anaesthesia. But *that* transition, on the operating table, I mean, it would just frighten you to death!

However, there are occasions for us in the West when we can use acupuncture anaesthesia. There are vast numbers of people who need surgery because they are going through tremendous pain and discomfort and suffering, and many times the surgeon may have to say, 'I am sorry, I can't operate because the condition of your heart is so bad'; or, 'The condition of your lungs is so bad that, if I administered the anaesthetic, the odds are that you would die from the anaesthetic, not the surgery.'

You may know people who are in that situation. So, in the West, we can offer them an alternative. Instead of them spending the rest of their life suffering, we may be able to use acupuncture anaesthesia for these cases. But, I think, for most people, we would rather stick to the normal Western methods—traditional to us.

So there is not really any great place for acupuncture anaesthesia in the Western world. Nor is there really any place at all for barefoot doctor in the Western world. They are very gimmicky. Traditional medicine is not like that at all.

The vast difference between traditional Chinese medicine and the methods I have just described is that traditional Chinese medicine *does not treat the symptoms*. And as we go on during the course of the day you will see the wisdom in this. You will see how sensible it is. And you will see how foolish it is to treat a symptom. Because a symptom really is a distress signal from the body or the mind or the spirit saying, 'Hey, for heaven's sake help me!' It is not the cause. It is the symptom saying, 'Help me, something has gone wrong!' So, how foolish for us just to treat the symptom, when the cause is left undisturbed.

It is a very in-depth, personal system of medicine. And to become a doctor of traditional Chinese medicine takes ten years of training. There is a vast difference between someone who does traditional Chinese medicine and someone who does local doctor, which you can probably learn in a few weeks.

So what I want to share with you today is some of the joys and the wisdom of traditional Chinese medicine. In so doing, I hope that you will be able to learn much about your own body, your own mind, and your own spirit. And then, like me, I am sure you will be tremendously impressed with the wisdom of the ancient Chinese. Because what I am going to share with you is nothing that I have discovered; I am just going to relate traditional Chinese medicine to you as it was written in the Nei Jing five thousand years ago. This system of medicine has not changed in five thousand years; and it will not change in the next five thousand years.

We in the West think, 'Wait a minute; there is something new every day.' But, when we go into this system of medicine, we find it is based on natural laws. I put it to you that neither man nor woman can improve upon Nature. This system of medicine is based on the most solid foundation of any system of medicine in the world. It is wholly based on natural laws. Man cannot pollute it; man cannot change it; man cannot improve upon it. Although it may be new in the Western world, one has to recognise that one quarter of the world's population has been treated by this system of medicine for over five thousand years. If it was not valid, then it would have died thousands of years ago.

One of the great joys about being a practitioner of traditional Chinese medicine is that it teaches us so much about ourselves, and about Nature. It brings us closer to Nature, closer to the real joy in life; and it gives us a sense of proportion. Thus we enrich our own lives by understanding more about our own bodies, minds and spirits.

In this traditional Chinese medicine, you will hear me use the words body, mind and spirit; but we are one. We consist of those three parts, which in total make one, make us.

A lot of people have difficulty when you mention the word 'spirit'. They think, 'Oh my God, he's going off his rocker. He's talking about some spiritual entity.' And other people say, 'Hey, wait a minute; he's on a religious crusade; he's talking about God.' This is one of the great tragedies of the Western world. You see, living in the twentieth century, we cannot say, 'This is the peak of civilisation.' It's a barbaric age we live in, because we are getting our sense of proportion wrong. We are leaving out the spirit.

We need to understand this system of medicine so that we can start to get our proportions right. If we were just body-mind, we would simply be robots. You can make something think and act and talk and move; but what makes *you* that unique, wonderful individual *you* are? What gives the quality to your life? What gives the spark to your life? What gives the ultimate joy and understanding and compassion? That is the spirit part of you, which makes you different from a robot. And as we go on, you will see how, in the West, we have lost our sense of proportion. If we see a mother with a little new-born child, we will turn round and say, 'How is the baby today?' She'll say, 'Oh wonderful; she's put on two pounds.' 'Oh, that is wonderful!' Next week, 'How is the baby?' 'Oh, put on another two pounds.' 'Wonderful!' Here you see we are measuring the baby's progress by the physical improvement.

A little later on, 'Is your baby at school now?' 'Yes.' 'Oh, how's he doing?' 'In the top grade.' 'Oh, how wonderful!' So now we are measuring the progress of the child by his or her mental capacity.

What about the most important part of the child? Do we ever go along and say, 'Hey, how's the spirit of the child?' Nobody mentions that. We are not measuring that. The child can grow bodily; the child can grow mentally. But are we trying to create a nation of robots who are ignoring the spirit which is the quality of themselves? This is why we are not winning the fight against disease.

There is more sickness today than there was fifty years ago, simply because we are abandoning and neglecting the most integral part of man and woman. If the spirit within us is deficient, we are much more susceptible to disease. The strength of each individual depends on his core. We have to talk a little here about Gods. Now I don't mean a specific God —I mean your own God, call it what you like. The Ultimate. The architect of the whole universe. He's not *out there*. You know how people go around on Sunday mornings, so the churches will be filled. And the preachers will be saying 'And now we will give thanks to God.' God must feel sick; they are doing it in such a monotonous tone. I would like to see some laughter there; that would fill his heart with joy. And they go, 'And God . . . '; but God's not up there! He is inside you. God is within each one of you. He is the spirit and the essence that is within you. Only people don't know that. In fact, we are an extension of the universe.

We are going to break the body up during the course of the day into five Elements. And we are going to break all of your organs up; and we are going to relate these organs to the natural elements outside. You are going to see that whatever happens naturally outside also happens within us. We are simply an extension of the cosmic energy.

Many people talk about vital Qi energy, the life force, and think it's enveloped within us. Really, it's just an extension of the ultimate source of energy which comes from the cosmos. We are part of that—the macrocosm and the microcosm.

And we will see too, if we have an organic imbalance inside us, how much it is influenced by the time of day, by the season of the year. We will understand why at certain times of the year we feel worse than at others: because we are an extension of that seasonal Element. Also, when that Element becomes imbalanced outside, then it is likely to cause an Elemental imbalance inside.

Do you know, a child of seven can understand the wisdom of traditional Chinese medicine? It's so simple; it's so basic; it's so natural. Yet we have turned our backs on it. We are now going in for things that isolate the body. You have a cardiac specialist; you have a pulmonary specialist; you have a kidney specialist. We are specialising in parts. We are not parts, we are one. And any one part of us that is not functioning correctly must affect the whole. The part that is affected is not necessarily the cause; it may only be the symptom.

As I go on to explain to you some of these very basic simple laws, you will see the wisdom of this system of medicine. How valid it is. And you will start to learn much about why you behave the way you do.

But before I really do start, I want to say to you first of all that I am not being facetious; I am being very honest. The great tragedy is that we neglect the natural gifts we are given when we were first born. I firmly believe that no man nor woman can be your teacher. I do not believe in gurus, at least not in the form of human beings. I feel that our teacher is Nature itself. Everything we want to know is out there in Nature.

If you want a teacher in physical form, then you must look at a child. A child below the age of one, who is not yet polluted, and trained, and regulated. You will see that, when we were born, we were given gifts that you can put no price on—and we were foolish enough to throw all these gifts away for material things. That's going to make you feel sad; but I hope then, what this talk may do, is help you spend some part of your life in resurrecting these gifts that you were once given.

For example, I am going to say to you, in all honesty, that I doubt whether any more than—no I won't even say one per cent, I'll make it total—I doubt whether *anyone* in this room can see more than fifty percent. You say, 'No, don't insult me, I can see.' Oh no, you can't see! You don't see; you don't use your eyes. Your eyes are really something . . . You never woke up this morning and said, 'Thank God, I can see.' You just said, 'So what?' You don't think enough about your eyes until perhaps they are threatened, until perhaps something happens to them; and then you are conscious you have got eyes. 'Oh my God, what's happening to my eyes?'

When you came here from A to B, from your residence or from wherever you were to come here, on the way you may have said, 'Did you see that?' 'Yes.' 'Did you see the flowers?' 'Yes.' ''Did you see the grass?' 'Yes.' 'Did you see that stone?' 'Yes.'

You didn't! No, you didn't! You took a cursory glance. You just used your eyes within a certain restricted perimeter. Your visions, your looking at life, at each other, at everything is through that restricted vision. We all have restricted vision. Simply because we haven't got time.

Now, what I would like you to do is to prove this to yourself. You may have just passed a rock. You say, 'Yes, a rock. I saw that rock.' Oh no, you didn't! You cursorily glanced at that rock. If you stopped and you looked at that rock, and the sun was shining, you would see a myriad of different reflections of lights. The whole thing would come alive.

You pick up a blade of grass, and you say, 'Well, there are millions of these.' But look at it and feel it; just look at it and become part of that blade of grass; and you say, 'My God, this is a miracle! Never seen anything so beautiful! I mean, the colour and the texture.' And then you pick up another blade of grass and say, 'My God, they are not the same!' Every blade of grass is different. But you didn't stop to see; you just had a cursory glance.

Stop and look at a plant. Stop and look at a tree. Look at a tree and you will break down, you'll cry. You will say, 'I have never seen such beauty!' But you haven't stopped to look at a tree. You've just looked at a tree and said, 'That's it.' Look at the sky. You say, 'Yes, I've seen the sky.' You haven't seen the sky. You stop and look at the sky and you could stay there all day. The multiplicity of changes; what it's trying to relate to you; and then it really becomes part of you. Now you can see.

Come back to human beings. We are looking at each

other with that same restricted vision. We are saying, 'Well, I saw Joe.' You didn't see Joe. You saw a physical body, and you said, 'Well, that's Joe.' But Joe is more than a physical body. Like the blade of grass is more than just something lying in a field; and the tree is something very individual; and so is Joe.

We are looking at each other and passing an opinion upon each other without looking beyond the physical body. The mind is more important than the physical body. And the spirit, that which emanates and radiates from an individual, is more important than that.

When you are looking at a tree properly, you must develop your sight. You must enlarge and remove the perimeters. It is all there for us to see, but we only choose to see part of it because we are in too much of a hurry. We only choose to see part of each other. Small wonder there is animosity and hatred and bitterness in the world. For goodness sake! We are all brothers and sisters; but we don't treat each other like that. We don't see each other as we really are. We only see that little bit we need to see. But if you can see the God, the spirit, in some other individual, then you will never have seen a more beautiful creature on the face of this earth than your own brother and sister. But how are you going to know that if you don't develop your sight so that you can see within a person? And then all the hatred and animosity goes by. You see a reflection of God, and your own image and their image within you, when you really look at a human being.

You may say, 'What's this got to do with Chinese medicine?' Well, those of you who have had an examination in traditional Chinese medicine will know it takes two to two-and-a-half to three hours. What we are trying to do is to get right within you, so we can see you as a unique individual from all three levels.

Having said that, there is not one man or woman on

the face of this earth who is anything like another. We say, 'men', 'women'. Ridiculous, there is no such thing as 'men'! There is no such thing as 'people'! Because each man and woman is a unique individual. They are as different as two blades of grass. They are as different as two different trees.

When you are treating someone who is sick you have got to understand how that unique individual functions. One of the joys of this system of medicine is that one never treats two people the same. So, if this young lady has a cough, and that young lady has a cough, they would both be treated entirely differently. Why? Because they are both unique individuals. Very different. Now you see where we fall into a trap in Western medicine (though I am not decrying Western medicine). We say, 'You take that, and you also take that.' But she gets better and she gets worse—with the same medicine.

Take a great drug like penicillin, which has saved many thousands of lives. Other people, it's made them deaf for the rest of their lives. One man's meat is another man's poison. So, with this system of medicine, we find out the unique needs of a person; and we fulfil those needs.

As I go on, you will find, too, that diet, exercise, many things play a very important part in the maintenance of a healthy body, mind and spirit. How many desperate people have made themselves even more sick by going on a diet; because there is no such thing as a general diet for all. What will make one person grow will destroy another. You come from different soils; you have different needs. Therefore, you will find that, once you can understand what it is the body needs, then you can tailor-make the diet for that person. But to have a gross overall diet can improve some people and can destroy others.

Now we see that we are unique individuals; and the physician must always look at us in that light. It's very, very fascinating. And you will see too how one person can have an illness and another person can have an almost identical illness. With the one person it can cripple him and put him into bed and he feels he wants to die; the other person can still carry on at work, although he has the same type of disease. This shows you the importance of the state of a person's mind and spirit in dealing with disease.

You will also find we lay far too much importance on physical pain, physical manifestations, and I put it to you that most people can tolerate a fair amount of physical pain. But you know what you can't tolerate—when it starts to get to your mind. When you get depressed, when you get worried, when you get anxious, when you get tense, when you can't sleep, when you get really irritable and really edgy, you feel within yourself you don't want to bother to carry on. That is worse. The mental anguish is worse than physical pain. And when you go deeper to the spiritual anguish, that's the time when you want to give up. It's not worth living—there's just no point in going on.

Another reason why we are not winning the fight against disease—going back perhaps a hundred, two hundred years ago, 'named' diseases (we don't name diseases in traditional Chinese medicine) like 'arthritis', 'lumbago' and 'rheumatism' were very often caused by people having to work outside, badly clothed, badly fed and badly housed. Being exposed to these unnatural conditions the outside elements affected the physical body. They got lumbago, rheumatism, torticollis. Now, at least in the West, everyone's pretty well housed, everyone is pretty well fed. If it rains and you have an outside job, now you can come inside. You don't have to work up to your knees in mud like they did a hundred years ago. You have all the facilities under the sun available. And yet there is still as much rheumatism and arthritis and torticollis as there was a hundred years ago. But the cause now is internal, not external. The disease is being caused now by worry, fear, grief, hostility, anger, hatred, jealousy: all of these are now manifesting in the physical body as rheumatism, etc.

When you have these two contexts, you can see how foolish it is to treat the rheumatism. One was caused by excessive damp, cold, standing in water, no ventilation, no warmth, bad clothing. Nowadays it is the internal factor. The hatred, the anger, the fear converts to aggressive energy, and then you manifest rheumatism, and you can't move your arms. How stupid to give a pill to cure it! One was caused by an outside factor; now it is caused by an inside factor.

Our job is to find the cause of the disease; so, in this case, we would try to find the internal cause of the rheumatism. Once we have established the cause we will try to correct it. If we can correct it, the rheumatism goes not for a day, not for a year, but forever. So the main thing in this system of medicine is first our ability to diagnose the cause of the disease.

Before we go on to that, we have to understand very, very loosely, how acupuncture really works. I am going to tell it to you in a very basic, simplistic way—which, as I said earlier on, a young child could understand.

It is stated in this system that in our body we have ten Organs and two Functions. This afternoon, if you are still with me and haven't gone home, I am hoping to share with you some of the understanding of one of the functions—Circulation-Sex.

The ten Organs are—your Heart, Small Intestines, Bladder, Kidney, Gall Bladder, Liver, Lungs, Colon, Stomach and Spleen. They are the ten Organs, and, in addition, the Chinese say you have two Functions—Circulation-Sex and Three Heater.

If these ten Organs and two Functions are working in

balance and harmony as Nature ordained, it is impossible— I will repeat that word, impossible—to be sick in body, mind or spirit. Every disease throughout the whole of the world is caused as a result of one or more of those Organs not functioning correctly. As the Organ (or those Organs) starts to go out of balance; then disease will be the result, either disease of the mind, or disease of the body, or disease of the spirit. And then you can give it a label! Now, isn't that a sweeping statement?

Basically, all that we have got to do is to correct the imbalance—bring these Organs as near to balance as we possibly can; and then the disease will disappear. Such a sweeping statement; but it is one hundred percent true.

How do we influence these organs? Well, each organ in our body has a meridian or a pathway going through it. And, along this meridian, flows vital Qi energy, or life force, call it whatever you wish. And it is this vital Qi energy that enables the organ to function. Now you say, 'Hey, wait a minute! I can't go along with this.' Well, let me just talk about the organ you all know, your heart. You all know that you've got a heart, don't you? Get a text book and it will tell you whereabouts it is. And you will see you have got this heart and it pumps—bump, bump, bump. You feel it sometimes; especially when you are in love; it goes faster!

So how does the heart function? Have you ever stopped to think? There is no such thing as perpetual energy. No such thing as perpetual motion—without a force to drive it. What do you think drives the heart?

Your lungs expand and contract. What do you think makes them expand and contract? It's the vital Qi energy that goes to those organs. Let me give you a simple analogy.

If you get the finest car engine in the world, which, of course, is the Rolls Royce—I get a commission for saying that by the way. There you have an engine that is manufactured to the ultimate. Now, you put it in a motor car and you can't even go down 57th Street unless you put some gas in the tank. Once you put the gas in the tank, and it's mixed with the right amount of air, then the engine will start to function, and you have a beautiful ride down the street.

If that mixture were too weak, although you still have the same beautiful engine, it will stop, start, stop, start, flutter. The engine can only function as well as the mixture of gas and air allows it to function. If you put aviation fuel in, that same engine would race and burn up. So you see, although the engine is important, what is even more important for the maintenance and smooth running of that engine, to last you 50, 150, 200,000 miles before it breaks down, is the mixture of air and gas.

Now, take your heart. You have, if you like, a fuel pipe which carries the gas and air which we are going to call Qi energy. So you have a meridian which comes from the inside of your little finger, goes across the palm of your hand, up the inside of your forearm, the inside of your arm, goes up your axilla, then it comes right over to the heart itself. It carries on down to your umbilicus—for those of you who don't like technical terms, belly-button (I like that one)—comes back up here by the side of your throat and up to your mouth, and it goes directly to your heart. Your heart can only function as well as that vital Qi energy will allow it to function.

Along that meridian there are certain acupuncture points. And let's relate those to a motor car again. If the mixture was too weak, the garage mechanic would make a little adjustment, and once he got the adjustment right, that engine would go beautifully—so traditional acupuncture is garage mechanics. We go into the acupuncture points and we can influence that Qi energy to balance it so that the heart that was racing can quieten down. The heart that was struggling to beat can now beat effortlessly. Hence the use of acupuncture points. That is the way that we influence the Qi energy to make that organ function as near normal as humanly possible.

On some meridians, we have as few as nine acupuncture points; on other meridians, we have as many as sixty-seven. In the whole of the body, we have about 360 points through which we can influence the energy which flows to any one of the twelve Organs in your body. And our effort is to try to get all of the twelve to come as near to balance as possible. Then we don't mind if you come suffering from cancer or a cough. If we can balance those twelve Organs, that disease will disappear. Isn't that a sweeping statement? But it's factual, it's truthful, and it's very, very simple to do —in a difficult sort of way.

So, how do we know whether the Organs are functioning as Nature ordained? I will show you the multiplicity of ways in which we can discover the distress signals that the body sends out.

You will have seen what I mean when I told you that you are half-blind, or you only half-see, you only half-hear, you only half-touch. Do you think that Nature is so vicious that one day you can go to bed full of the joys of spring, and the next day you get up with pneumonia, or pleurisy or bronchitis? No, Nature doesn't do that. Nature's very, very kind. Nature will warn you six months, nine months, twelve months before you get the disease and say something is going wrong. But we are so blind, we are so deaf, we are so dumb, that we don't take any notice, and we don't see until it is too late.

The joy of traditional Chinese medicine is that it is a preventive system of medicine. If you went to a doctor at the change of every season and he was able to make a diagnosis as soon as he felt that some part of one of the Organs was slightly imbalanced, he would correct the imbalance, thus preventing disease. Doesn't that sound sensible?

What do we do with our motor cars? We buy a brand new motor car and have to take it in one day for an oil change, or take it in for a check. You will check the plugs, you will do this, you will do that. Why? So that the car will go on giving you beautiful service. The garage mechanic says, 'Hey, wait a minute; you had better get that big end seen to; it's knocking.' You will say, 'Right, will you do it? How much does it cost?', and pay it.

Now, if I was going along the streets and said to somebody, 'Wow! You had better come and let me treat you because in the space of about another two months you are going to have a heart attack,' they would say, 'Are you trying to bloody rip me off? . . . I mean, I don't mind spending $100 on my car because the mechanic told me it is going to break down, but you don't come to me with that rubbish that my body is going to break down. I will wait until it breaks down first, then I'll believe you.' It works out that we are putting more credence in material things; yet that is the most precious gift ever put on the face of the earth—*a human being.*

So, the beauty of this system of medicine is that we can pick up the distress signals as Nature tells us. Nature tells us not once, but about five different ways, the minute any Organ starts to imbalance, sending our distress signals saying, 'Hey, get this seen to.' Because we don't see, we don't look, we don't hear, we don't feel, we ignore the message. Do you know that every time any Organ in your body malfunctions the colour on your face changes?

Now you start looking at each other and say, 'Well, yes, I can see. He's red, he's white.' But I don't mean the general overall colour. In certain areas of your face the moment an Organ malfunctions, a colour change comes immediately, and stays there.

One of the great difficulties of the students when they come to the College is that it may be one year, may be two years, or three years, or perhaps even more, before they can develop their sight so that they see those colours when they are there. That shows you how restricted our vision is. They have to develop their sight so that they can see what is already there.

A child can see it. So could you when you were little. But have you really spent any time in your developing years developing this God-given gift? No, you have neglected it. My God! You don't just see with your physical eye, you see with your mind's eye. People say, 'Do you see what I mean?' Well, of course, you don't physically see what they mean, but you do see 'inside' what they mean. Seeing with the mind's eye is another deeper way of seeing than with the physical eye. But seeing with the eye of your own spirit, the spirit of someone else, is the deepest vision of all. You see what I mean by saying that we are half blind? We can't even see this colour until we re-develop our sight. I will find a graduate like Richard here, can turn round and say, 'Hey, J.R., I can see those colours as plain as day.' And yet seven years ago he would say, 'Are you trying to pull my leg saying there is a colour there?' And that's how much his sight has developed since. And many of the practitioners in this room will tell you that is true.

Secondly, the minute an Organ becomes imbalanced in your body, your body emits an odour. Don't move away from each other because you can't even half-smell! I mean, if you could, then you wouldn't sit where you are!

An odour is emitted from your body the minute an Organ starts to malfunction. Now, isn't it marvellous that nature does this to us? And yet we are so bunged up that we can't discern it. You know that this is true when disease has fully manifested. Those of you who have anything to do with medicine know that in the old days when T.B. was rife, you only had to walk in the door and you could smell T.B., you could smell death. You go into a room where a child is having a raging fever. You can smell the fever when it's really bad. But if you were smelling correctly you could smell that imbalance, that impending disease, three months before it manifested.

Do you know that the minute an Organ imbalances in your body, your emotions change? 'Emotions,' you say; 'What the hell are those?' We are going to talk about them because it's really wonderful to know about them. Then you will see why we behave like we do. Not by choice, but because the Organs in your body determine it. You don't control it. The Organs in your body control it.

Furthermore, we have six pulses on one hand and six pulses on the other. Each relates to one of the Organs. And the minute there is an imbalance in one of the Organs you can feel it, when you are 'taking pulses'.

This is another thing that students go through. They first of all say, 'I can't feel anything.' That's because they haven't developed the God-given sensitivity in their hands. Watch a baby. A baby doesn't even have to touch. A baby at a distance can feel shapes, sizes, vibration. And then what do we do with this precious gift? We just abuse it. Never bother to say, 'I can feel, I can feel!' You've got to spend a few years developing, re-developing this. Then you can discern the twelve pulses. Then you can say, 'Oh, now I can physically feel—there is an imbalance on an Organ!'

Also when there is an imbalance on any Organ in your body, your voice changes. You say, 'What do you mean my voice changes?' Your voice *changes*. Your voice is controlled by the Organs, not by you. We will go into that.

So we have colour. We have smell. We have the pulses. We have the emotions and we have the voice. Changes in these will take place six months, nine months, or a year before you actually get the disease. That's how kind Nature is. Nature keeps telling you, 'Something is going wrong, something is going wrong, something is going wrong.' But we don't look. We don't see. We don't feel. We wait until we have got the disease and then say, 'We are sick.'

This is one of the joys—being able to prevent disease. Of course, in the Western world, most of the patients we get are patients who are discarded by other systems of medicine. A physician may say, 'I am sorry, we can't do anything more for you. I am sorry, you will have to stay on these drugs for the rest of your life.' Those patients are the people that generally come to us to seek our aid. And even though they come—shall we say, right at the wrong end of the spectrum, in many cases—with the grace of God, we are able to restore the balance of these Organs, and thus the disease can disappear. And that is very beautiful.

Now, wouldn't it be worthwhile if we understood a little more about these odours and these emotions and these sounds? This then might tell us why we behave like we do ourselves, and, more particularly, why those very close to us are suddenly changing their behaviour.

You see often that a man may be with a woman and they might be quite ecstatic. Then suddenly the woman will say, 'I don't know what's happened to my husband. When he comes home from work now, he's that bloody irritable. He kicks the cat. Got not time to look at the kids. If his dinner's not on the table he starts raving. He never used to be like that. If you get him in company you have got to watch what he is saying, otherwise he will upset the apple cart. He's totally changed.' That's the disease.

He doesn't want to be like that. Who on earth wants to be like that? But many people are like that. And you will see as we go along that if you have an imbalance on the Element Wood, which controls your anger, your anger becomes imbalanced. You don't control it. That, too is a distress signal from the body saying, 'Now can you see you need help?' But no; we have to wait until a person gets hepatitis or psoriasis, or a liver disease, or gallstones. Then we recognise that there is a Wood imbalance; and by then, in many cases, it is too late.

So what am I going to tell you after you have had a cup of coffee? (It's not really because you want a cup of coffee. I see some of you are dying for a cigarette. Nipping out of the door one at a time wanting a cigarette. Just shows again the imbalance, but it's a healthy sort of imbalance that I enjoy myself). What I am going to do when you come back, if you come back, is to start talking about the Five Elements, and the basic laws within the Five Elements. And, by golly, you are really going to know how you function, and why you function like you do; and we are going to have a lot of fun on the way!

What we normally do, at this point, is appoint a Supreme Controller. You know, we normally have a God, a King. Everybody likes to be God or a King. So, what we are going to do is pick the strongest person, before whom you are all likely to shudder in fear. So we are going to make you the Supreme Controller. All right? (J.R. picks out a member of the audience). And you can give these people a given amount of time; and then they have to be back when you say. Is that fine? How long do you want? . . . Good, glad to see you in five minutes. That's healthy. Now, what we will do, because it's Sunday, and to show you we love you and we are compassionate, we will give you six. So if you are back in your seats within six minutes we will kick off with something about traditional acupuncture. O.K.?

After Coffee

Here, on the chart *(on opposite page)*, we have the red Element Fire. And you notice that within Fire we have two Organs, the Heart and the Small Intestines. We also have the two Functions, Circulation-Sex and Three Heater. Those constitute the Element Fire.

Next, we have the yellow Element Earth; the Stomach and the Spleen are situated in the Earth Element. Then the white is the Element Metal, where we have the Lungs and the Colon. Next the blue represents Water, where we have the Bladder and Kidneys. Finally the green represents the Liver and Gall Bladder, which makes up the Element Wood.

You can see, each of the circles is joined to the next by a line which travels round in a clockwise direction: and that is the way the vital Qi energy travels throughout the whole of your body, mind and spirit, from the moment of birth until you die. The energy goes round from one Organ, one Element to the other, in a continuous circle.

Here we see that we have many things that we can already interpret from the Elements themselves.

First of all, the Element Fire represents the summer. Summer is the very beautiful time of the year when we can discard some of our superficial clothing and let the sun come on our bodies, and feed and encourage us. Then there

The Five Elements

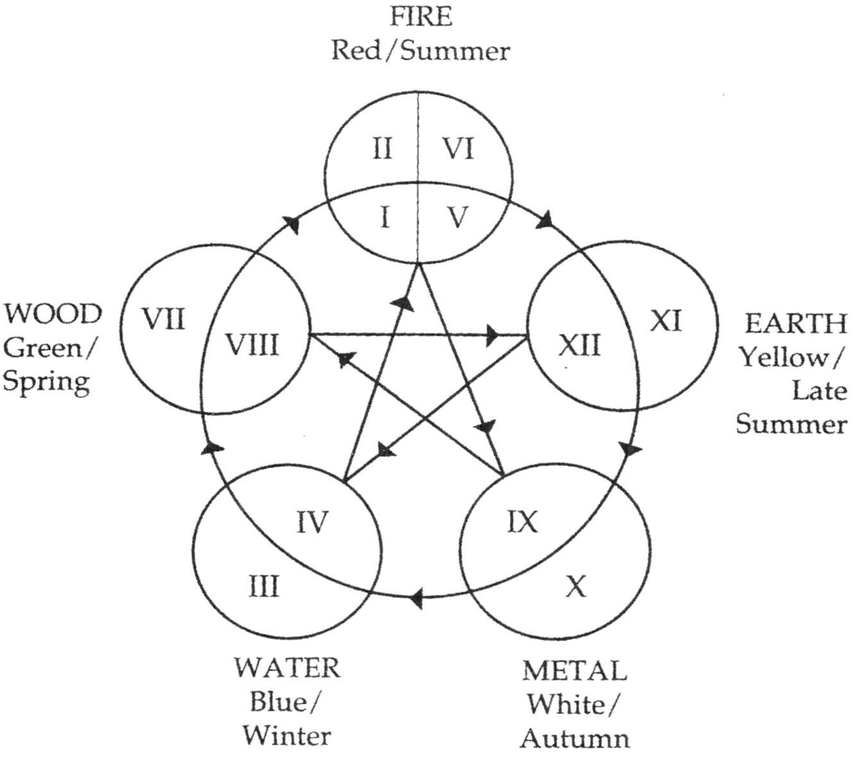

I -	Heart	VII -	Gall Bladder
II -	Small Intestines	VIII -	Liver
III -	Bladder	IX -	Lung
IV -	Kidney	X -	Colon
V -	Heart Protector	XI -	Stomach
VI -	Three Heater	XII -	Spleen

comes a time, a little later on, when we welcome the late summer, when the evenings get a little cooler. And the late summer, again, has some warmth and a gentle breeze, a very beautiful time of the year.

We follow on to the fall, or autumn as we call it at home, and this too is a magnificent time of the year when Nature shows a multiplicity of colours. Everything now is falling from the trees and returning to the earth from whence it came.

And then we have the winter, which again is another lovely time of the year, where there is a stillness. Not so much activity. Just a quiet period. The Lord in his wisdom at some stage during the winter will cover everybody's front garden with six inches of snow so that all our gardens are the same. It is a great time of levelling.

Then we have the spring, which is a magnificent time of the year. The season of birth and growth—and they tell me then a young man's fancy turns to love. There's a lightness in his step, and, 'Hey, spring is coming!'

There are five seasons in which anyone who is reasonably well balanced in their body, mind and spirit can feel at ease, comfortable. Be grateful for each of those seasons.

But, if you have an imbalance—shall we say, for example, in the Liver and the Gall Bladder, that is the Element of Wood, which is governed by the season of spring—then you will hate the spring. Or you will love the spring; 'Oh, that's the favourite time of the year.' How can you have a favourite when you have got five beautiful distinct seasons, each giving us something new and something fresh?

If you have a major imbalance in the Element Water— the Bladder and the Kidneys—you will detest the winter. 'God, I can't stand the winter.'

Did you realise that even a simple clue like that is one way in which the body is telling you, 'Wait a minute; there is something malfunctioning in your Kidney and Bladder.'

Then you get other people who say, 'I hate the sun. I can't stand the sun. I feel much worse in the sun.' If you have an imbalance in the Heart or Small Intestines, Circulation-Sex or Three Heater, then you will either love the sun—oh, and worship it—or you will go the opposite way and detest it.

Do you realise that Nature is giving you these warnings? That if you have a slight imbalance on any Organ, it will affect you seasonally? So now if you suddenly find where 'Gosh; I used to like the summer, now I hate it!', heed the distress signal that is coming from your body, mind and spirit. Because, if you have an imbalance in the Fire Element, you will hate the heat. Don't wait until you get a cardiac malfunction, or some serious malfunction of the Small Intestines, or some sexual malfunction, which will ultimately follow. Find out why it is that you can't live in accordance with the seasons, when they each have something very special to offer. A little baby could understand that; but did you realise that your body gives you that message? Don't ignore it. Say, 'Hey, why am I functioning like this? What is happening?' And you will find that one of the Organs which resides in that Element associated with that season is giving you a distress signal; something is wrong. You see how very, very simple that is.

That's one warning that Nature will give you that you yourselves, without any experience, can interpret. I am not going to ask you to put up your hands; I am sure there must be some people in this room who could say, 'When I go back five, six, seven years, I know I used to love going in the sun; I used to love going in the water; now I can't stand it.'

O.K.? That change is simply because you have an organic imbalance that is now starting to deteriorate. If you correct that imbalance, then you will go back to not loving one season more than the other, but feeling very much at peace, and very much at home, in each one of the seasons.

But, imbalanced, you get a seasonal malfunction, which is a result of a malfunction of an Organ that resides inside the appropriate Element.

The laws that are contained within the Five Elements are The Law of Mother/Child, The Law of Midday/Midnight, The Law of Husband/Wife, The Law of Cure and The Law of Five Elements. Those are the natural laws which I was telling you about this morning; and they will never alter.

If we can understand these laws, then not only can we understand more about ourselves, but we can more easily understand the people around us. Our own brothers and sisters.

A little later on, when we come to study the Fire circle, you will see why disease is greater today than it has ever been at any time since this earth was created. In spite of the advances we have made in living, in housing, in food, the incidence of disease is growing. I venture to suggest that perhaps in two generations from now there will be so many mentally disturbed people that there won't be enough mentally sane people to look after them; unless we can halt this stupid negligence towards our own bodies, minds and spirits, and pay more attention to them than to the new curtains, the new car, the new carpet, status, the new position, and all the things of this sort that don't bring joy and don't bring fulfilment.

One thing that is lacking today more than at any other time is Fire. It seems that we are putting out our own fires, as it were. The Element Fire, which is associated with the summer, is governed by the Heart, Small Intestines, Circulation-Sex and Three Heater. This Element represents love, joy, compassion, understanding, forgiveness. Now those are five beautiful-sounding words. I don't care what you tell me you want, I will tell you that the greatest thing you all need—no, want—more than anything else in the world, is to be loved and to love someone else.

If you can put a priority above that, then I am not going to believe you, because you really, really need it. It's the fuel for your life. If you have an imbalance in the Fire Element, then as your Fire starts to go out, you will find that you have not got that ability to love someone else. You haven't got the ability to love yourself. You cannot be forgiving, compassionate nor understanding.

How many people do you see whose life really is barren, because there is no Fire in their lives? There is no one to love, and they don't even love themselves.

If you have an imbalance on any one of those four Officials, or four Organs, that reside in the Fire Element, it will affect your ability to love. How many people do you know who at one stage—and perhaps you went through it yourself—seemed to have a tremendous love for all things and everyone, and then suddenly they said, 'Keep away from me. Don't touch me. I can't stand it. I don't want anyone near me.' If any of you have gone through that stage you will find that, again, is another distress signal.

How tragic for someone to go through life with their Fire going out. What is the point in going through life if you can't love anybody? Or if no one loves you? I mean, we are still children; that's another thing that you have to remember. It's good to get rid of this silly image we have that we are grown up. More wisdom from the early Chinese. A lot of disease is caused because we are trying to be grown up. We are trying to be men and women. 'I will do my own thing.' Rubbish! We are children.

Do you remember when you were a little child, and you depended upon your physical mother to feed you? To love you? How you depended upon your physical father to guide you? To protect you? To comfort you? And then came the day, sure, when you left your physical mother and father. But do you still remember that you are only alive *now* because of Mother Earth, Nature? Mother Earth who feeds you. When your human mother stops, right until the day you die, Mother Earth provides the food that you eat. Your Father 'above' provides the air you breathe, and there are we, children in between. Who wants to grow up? I love my natural Mother and Father like I love my physical mother and father. That gives me a sense of proportion. Now it's giving me respect.

When I get up in the morning, I thank God that I have got a Father and Mother to care for me, because without my Mother I am going to starve; and without my Father for four minutes I am going to die. The air that I breathe provided by him, and the food that I eat from my Mother, gives me life. So, truly, I want to respect my Mother and Father.

You see how we, now, in the twentieth century show our respect to our Mother? We build ruddy great skyscrapers on her stomach. We build great runways for airports on her stomach. We have lost all respect for her. Some day we have got to get that respect back again, else she will suddenly belch one day, and the earth will open and the buildings will come down. What a way to treat the provider who cares for us! How do we lose respect for Nature? Because it's easy. You go in the superstore, or the supermarket, and you think the bloody stuff grows in tins. It comes from Mother Nature, whatever they do with it before we get it. But do you really stop and think in the morning, 'Thanks Mum.' You used to say it to your real mother, I hope. Well start saying it to Mother Nature. And you say, 'Hey, thanks Dad.' Or do you just take it for granted that he is going to keep giving you this breath all the time? See how we are respecting that. We are polluting the very air that he provides us with. So we have got to come back to having more respect for our real Mother and Father who make life possible.

If we look here (on the diagram) we will see that the Stomach and the Spleen represent the Earth. This is our Mother. We have seen how important our Mother outside is to provide the food that we eat. So is our Mother inside to process the food that we eat. And if our Mother inside becomes sick, then we are like little children who have lost our mothers.

Just think of the thousands of symptoms that can arise from this. What happens to a little child whose mummy takes him down, say, into the middle of New York, and then lets the child's hand go? The child goes berserk. It can get paralysed. It can feel rejected. It can feel isolated. The child becomes unstable. The child will urinate with fear. It may defecate with fear. It may tremble with fear. The child may go hysterical. That's what you do if your Mother Earth inside your body becomes imbalanced and loses control of you.

Therefore you will see that we still have the manifestation within us of the dependency upon our mother to feed us. As we go along I will show you how these two Organs, Stomach and Spleen, really work.

We can see (on the diagram) how each of the Organs resides within an Element, each Element having two Organs, with the exception of Fire which has four. What happens is that the Qi energy travels round from one Element to the other, from the moment of birth until death. The Element Water, for instance, will pass on the vital Qi energy, the life force, to the Element Wood. You know that because Water helps to create Wood; without Water the Wood would perish. Water creates it.

Then we see that the Wood passes on the energy to Fire. Wood creates Fire. We know that. And then we see how the Fire passes the energy on to the Earth. Fire creates the Earth from the ashes. You see how the Earth creates Metal because the Metal is within the bowels of the Earth.

Then we see how Metal creates Water. Were there not Metal in the bowels of the Earth, the Water could not be collected to go into the reservoirs. It would fall straight through to the other side of the world.

So we find that this is a very natural cycle where the energy is passed on from one Element to create the next. To promote it; to preserve its well-being.

Now let's have a look at The Law of Mother/Child and see how the Chinese were able to put this in beautiful, simple, realistic language.

They said that, if you have a healthy mother, a healthy physical mother, and she has her newborn child, then the mother will put the child to her breast and will feed the child with the right volume and the right quality of milk, and will feed the child with love. Lesson number one: man or woman does not live by food alone. To love is as important, or perhaps more important, than the milk that the child has. If a mother was to feed a child with milk and no love, the child would not thrive. You see the wisdom, the recognition again, from five thousand years ago, how love is an integral part of growth and well being.

So, the natural healthy mother cradles the child in her arms and feeds the child from the breast with the right quality milk, the right volume, and lots of love. That child will thrive. Nothing wrong will happen to that child.

But let's suppose that we have a sick mother, and let us suppose that the milk is of very poor quality. Let us suppose that there isn't sufficient milk for the child to drink. Let us suppose that the mother is feeling so sick at that moment that she cannot give that little extra hug of love to the child, but just holds her arms there, saying, 'Oh, I wish she would hurry up and finish.' The child picks that up in a second. So the child is deprived of love, deprived of the quality of milk, deprived of the volume of milk.

What is going to happen with the child? It is going to scream its head off; it's going to yell; it's going to kick up tantrums; it's going to shout. What is the point of the doctor going to the child and saying, 'Ah, dear little diddums, what a shame!' The child will say, 'You fool. Can't you see the cause of the trouble?' So you go to the mother and say, 'Hey mum, what's happening? You are responsible. Nature ordains you would feed and look after the child.' And the mother says, 'But I am so sick.' So you build up the mother, and as you build up the mother she gets healthier. Then she picks up her child, and the child immediately quietens down because it has the right volume of milk, the right quality of milk, and the love again.

You may say, 'Hey, wait a minute. What's this got to do with me?' Again, the unbounded wisdom of the Chinese. They said that the Element Wood is the mother of the following Element which is Fire. So we will break it down a little. They say that the Liver in the Element Wood is mother of the Heart in the Element Fire. Now you will see how we are going wrong in Western thinking. Here we have a sick mother— we mean the Liver—that is responsible for passing the vital Qi energy. Remember I said that in the creative cycle, Wood creates Fire. We have a Wood imbalance, a sick mother, that cannot pass on the vital Qi energy to the Heart, to the child. So instead of the physical child screaming, the elemental child will scream. That means you are going to get a lot of cardiac distress signals. Pain in the heart, cardiac pain, irregularity of heart.

Now we are going to extend this vision of the Heart. Pains down the arm. Pins and needles in the arm. Inability to clench your fist—we are going to call that 'rheumatism' in a minute. 'Oh, I can't pick things up.' Doctors are going to say 'rheumatism'. But it is the child screaming because the mother's sick and is getting no energy. Also notice the meridian which comes up here. What happens when you feel panic-stricken? Your heart almost stops. You can't get the words out. If you get an imbalance of the Heart, also you get impediment of the speech. You get the inability to sound your words. You seize up. You may get a swollen throat or an infection of the throat and this then is called 'tonsilitis', 'pharyngitis', 'laryngitis'. These are just simply labels, or a symptom which would then be treated in isolation. You may also get pains around the heart, and again this can be labelled as 'angina'; or pains coming under your heart and this may be attributed to gas; and yet all of these symptoms are distress signals from the child saying, 'Come on! Come on! Something is happening. Something is going wrong.'

The Western-trained person, in the vast majority of cases, goes to the symptom or the child, then starts to treat either the heart or the throat. But the ancient Chinese would say, 'Wait a minute, let us find out why the Heart is sending out these distress signals.'

So the first thing we do is trace back and look at the mother. Here we see that the Liver is malfunctioning, thus unable to take care of its child. We go to the Liver. We increase the energy and make the Liver, the mother, balanced and well. We don't touch the Heart at all. Every one of those Heart symptoms disappears.

You see how Western medicine is specialising in the organic distress signals, when really what it should be doing is finding out why we are getting that distress signal. Doesn't that make sense? The Law of Mother/Child. It happens in real life; it happens within us.

Now this picture becomes a little more complicated; yet still in essence very simple. The Heart is the mother of the Spleen, and the Spleen is the mother of the Lungs. So, if you get asthma, pleurisy, you can't breathe. Instead of running to the Lungs, first go and see what is happening to the mother, the Spleen. It's not our job to pass on the vital Qi energy to create Metal. We can't do this, only Nature can do this. The Earth creates the Metal, not us. So, if we go back and treat the mother Earth, the Spleen, we don't have to touch the Lungs; and the bronchitis, broncho-emphysema, pneumonia, pleurisy, asthma—all of these silly labels—all disappear.

Now can you understand the dangers of a local doctor? With local doctor treatment, if you had a pain in the heart, they would get out their 'cook-book' and it will say 'heart pain; use Heart Point 7.' If they sedate Heart 7, the pain will diminish, but it must come back again; and so you go back to the local doctor and they diminish the pain again. And while they are doing this, the mother is becoming more sick, and more sick, and more sick. They're ignoring the cause and palliating the symptom. Small wonder that the next time you get a pain in the heart, the odds are it will be a heart attack. Because they have ignored the cause of the disease and have been playing about with the surface symptom. They have been trying to placate the child with a bottle, and the bottle is no substitute for a natural mother. Isn't that simple, and very wise?

It doesn't stop there—if you are still with me. The Lung is then the mother of the Kidney, the Kidney is the mother of the Liver. Each Organ in turn, at one stage, becomes the mother and, in the next stage becomes the child. Isn't this the way Nature ordained? You were the child of your mother, and then one day you may be the parent of your child. And that is how we all are. If the law was not in existence we would not be here. The wisdom of the Chinese is unbelievable. I think it was the peak of civilisation—that they understood such laws. And we have let it go to waste. We must resurrect it; it's so important.

Now I want to carry the family situation on a little bit further. Liver is the mother, Heart the child. The Kidney is the grandmother of the Heart, or the mother of the Liver. Are you with me? O.K.

Let us assume that the Heart's mother is sick; that is the Liver. So we are going to get the symptoms from the child, the Heart. Now you are going to get grandmother worrying about her grandchild. You have got to be a grandmother or a grandfather to realise this! When you have got your own children at home, sure you worry about them, but you are there. You are in control.

Now my daughter rings me up and says, 'Dad, Russell's not very well' (that's my grandson). I say, 'Well, are you doing this, are you doing that, are you doing the other?' She says, 'Don't be stupid Dad, of course I am. 'She's a complete mother, but I see her as my child still. Then I think, 'Is Hilary doing this for Russell? Is she doing that?' And so I go to bed at night. 'Oh my God, I wonder how Russell is?' He's not there; I can't see him; and I am thinking the worst; and all of a sudden I find I cease to function. So my daughter phones up and says, 'Where's Dad?' 'Oh, Dad, he's not very well.' 'What's wrong with him?' 'Well I don't know.' And then later my wife says to her, 'Oh, by the way, how's Russell?' Then my wife comes up to see me. 'How's Russell?' I say. She answers, 'Oh, he's fine.' I'm up. Good. Wait until you are a granny or a grandad; you think, 'What's happening?' That's natural. That, as God is my judge, is natural. And it is natural within *you*.

I have shown a situation where you will get heart malfunctions because of a sick mother, but you might well get kidney diseases showing. Frequency of urination, oedema of the legs, kidney pain, inability to pass water, cystitis, swelling underneath the eyes. All manner of diseases associated with Water. And they say, 'My God, let's go and treat the Kidneys.' You must be joking! You treat the Liver which is the cause of the disease; the minute that puts the Heart right, then the grandmother, the Kidney stops worrying. So you see it isn't as simple as Mother/Child. That is why we have to examine every Organ in your body to find out the cause. It is no good our treating the grandmother; that won't make the grandchild better, especially if the cause is related to the mother. See, it's simple; and yet it now becomes complicated, in a very nice sort of way. But, to find out which is the cause, we are going to know by the colour, we are going to know by the sound, we are going to know by the odour, we are going to know by the emotions, and we are going to know by the sound of the voice. That is going to tell us the cause of the disease.

Many patients who come to us, and those of you who have had an examination will realise this is so; you others may think it is weird! 'I came in here with a ruddy pain in my arm, and he wants to know what diseases I had when I was seven years of age. He wants to know all that has happened to me. He wants to know whether my birth was easy. He wants to know if I have had any inoculations, vaccinations, previous surgery, previous diseases' (because most diseases today are not cured, they are suppressed). Yes, it does seem weird at first!

Now I am going to share a very simple example of suppression with you. Each one of you in the room will know somebody, one of your friends, who fits into this category. This friend—who has bronchitis, asthma, bronchial emphysema, any major chest trouble—you go back and ask them if, when they were younger, they had acne or eczema; and seven or eight out of every ten will have. And you say, 'Well, what did you do for it?' And they will say, 'I got some cortisone cream and it went.'

In Chinese medicine you have three lungs—these two here in the chest, and your skin. If you don't breathe through your skin, you will die, just as much as if you don't breathe through your lungs. Why don't we recognise that this is our third lung? It helps to oxygenate the blood, it helps to get rid of the impurities and the toxins and the poisons, and it needs to breathe. Otherwise we are shut off from the cosmic energy. We would die inside. We are an extension of the cosmic energy.

Therefore, before you get a major disease deep within the two lungs, in ninety-nine cases out of every hundred the first distress signals will be on your skin. So if you get acne, or eczema, or psoriasis, and you suppress it by putting on a cortisone cream, you are driving that disease deeper.

It won't be one month before you get bronchitis, or your pleurisy, or your asthma. It might be five years, it might be ten, it might be fifteen, it might be twenty, but you will get it before you die, because you have driven that disease deeper into the economy of the mind.

So why do we ignore the distress signal? Why do we create so many serious chest disorders by simply trying to suppress a superficial thing that probably shows on your body when you are a youngster—nine, eleven, fifteen, twenty, early days—saying, 'Oh, I must get rid of this'? Cortisone cream should be banned, because it is sweeping the filth and the dirt underneath the carpet.

This is what we are doing with many diseases. You get, say a fever. I know, it's very frightening. 'Oh, his temperature is 103 degrees! Give him something to bring it down.'

Lord, give me a fever and I can cure anything! The fever is your body's own natural resources driving out and burning up the invading enemy. We are so scared, as soon as the temperature starts to go up to 103 degrees; we drop it, thus stopping the body from doing its own healing process. A fever is the greatest healing process in the world, if you let it come out.

Why would we panic because we go to 103 degrees? You won't die. But now we have been trained to bring a fever down. We have been trained to suppress that disease which would otherwise have been eliminated; and so we are going to pay for it later on. Hence the higher incidence of cardiac malfunctions through suppressing the Fire, rather more than letting it come out.

Here we can see again, in certain types of medicine, what we are doing is not curing but palliating for the time being, and then we must pay for it later on.

For heaven's sake, don't think I am entirely decrying Western medicine! There are millions of people alive today who would be dead were it not for the skill and expertise of Western medicine. I don't want you ever, either, to think I am totally decrying drugs. Drugs can be valuable. If you were to get involved in an accident you would thank God the doctor came along and gave you a pain killer; otherwise you would probably go berserk. You couldn't stand the pain. But then he takes you into hospital and *we* start the mending procedure; then you don't need the drugs.

Someone loses someone near and dear to them and, of course, they can't sleep. If they don't sleep, they are going to go out of their mind. The grief and the worry. So the doctor says, 'O.K.; take a few sleeping tablets.' Fantastic. Just gives the body, mind and spirit a chance to recuperate. *Then* you don't want your sleeping tablets. Only to help you over the crisis. But orthodox Western medicine has become such that, in my country, there are six million people taking sleeping tablets every single night, and they have done this for periods of five years. That's not medicine that's drug abuse. If you can't sleep, there is a reason. There is a cause why you can't sleep. It's a natural function; so it could be a distress signal. A person coming to us says, 'I can't sleep.' 'Why can't you sleep; it's natural?' We don't say, 'Take this to sleep'; we say, 'Why can't you?'

Then we find the cause why they can't sleep and endeavour to correct that; then they start sleeping. So drugs are useful in a given set of circumstances; but drug abuse by continually giving a dose is an excuse to say, 'Get out of my way; I'm not bothered. Just take these and keep out of my hair.' *My* hair! I mean, I haven't got much! But that bit I have got, keep out of it! That is not medicine; not as it was really meant to be practised.

This first Law, The Law of Mother/Child: this means that, when we get a disease of the mind and body and spirit screaming out saying, 'Hey, something is wrong', we don't go to that symptom, we have to find out the cause in the mother, or the grandmother, or wherever it is stemming from. Once we can establish where it stems from, then we can cure the disease. That is why we want to know so much about you, because your disease may have started when you were seven, and been suppressed, and suppressed and suppressed, and is now rearing its ugly head twenty years later.

You see then, what an important period your childhood is. We want to know your relationships with your Mum and Dad, with your brothers and sisters. You may say, 'Hell, what's that got to do with my arm? I have only come because I can't move my arm. Then you sit there and ask me about my sister. Damn her! Didn't like her in any case!' The odds are that that was the cause of the trouble! Because then you see there was so much jealousy—Daddy loved your sister. You were trying to compete with your sister, and hated her guts. Instead of living normally, your life as a child was contained, trying to compete with your sister. Trying to win the love of your father. An unnatural situation.

Then you can get a tremendous anger coming within the child, or a suppression of anger. You hear children say, 'I hated my mother!' Why did you hate the mother? And it comes out that they get an imbalance in the Element Wood, and they cease to grow. And then you suddenly find that an arm will stick, or a neck will stick, or their vision will be affected. And the cause of it was the malfunction caused on the Element Wood when the child was seven or eight. At some later stage in life, there may be a trauma, which then brings all this back up again, and then it manifests itself in the form of disease. So it is very important for us to know all this information. Relationships are tremendously important. You know we are, by and large, a very emotional group of people. We relate emotionally, and you can read someone's state of health, of each of those Officials, just by talking to them and seeing how they react emotionally.

Every one of those Elements is associated with an emotion. The Element Wood—Liver and Gall Bladder—is associated with the emotion of anger. Fire is associated with joy; Earth is associated with sympathy; Metal is associated with grief; Water is associated with fear. So there are five emotions that we all exhibit in a given set of circumstances.

Sure, there is a time when we get angry. We say, 'Get out of my bloody way!'; and then think, 'Oh, I wish I hadn't said that.' That's O.K.; you level out. And there is a time when it is great to be joyous—like our laughing this morning. That's wonderful! Some people haven't laughed in years. If they tried, their ruddy faces would crack. 'I don't laugh; what the bloody hell have I got to laugh about?' What the hell is living if you can't laugh? There is too little laughter in their life. That is because fires are going out. People now don't get the joy they used to get. Laugh more, and be more joyous, and we would be a healthier group of nations.

Someone comes along and puts their arm around you, and says, 'It's O.K. love; don't worry.' God, that's so supportive just at that time. But that's enough. Don't sort of fawn all over me; but, at that time, that sympathy is really needed. 'Don't worry, my sweetheart; it will be all right.' Just hold them. Natural.

Grief. We all exhibit the emotion grief. One day you have to lose your own mum and dad and, God, that's unbelievable. There is a hole there, and you grieve for them. As time goes on, you can talk about your mum and dad without crying and without breaking down, because Nature then has levelled you back out again. Then you only grieve in a given set of circumstances.

Fear. Sure, we all exhibit the emotion fear. I mean, if we didn't, we would walk straight in front of a bus. So fear is necessary; and we exhibit fear in a given set of circumstances.

But, if you have an imbalance on any of those Elements that control these emotions, the emotions become imbalanced. I want you to remember—I am not saying you *might* become imbalanced; I'm not saying imbalances appear in nine people out of every ten; I am saying imbalances happen with *every* human being on the face of this earth. What can be more secure and stable than that?

Let's look at fear first of all. If you have a major imbalance here, two things will happen with all of these emotions. One, you over-exhibit them; or, the other, you do not exhibit them at all, which is unnatural. So, you can get the sort of fear where, if you have a major imbalance on the Water Element, it reaches the point where you dare not go out of the house. You are so frightened that you dare not meet people. People get so frightened that they dare not go into an elevator. We call it agoraphobia or claustrophobia, all of these stupid sounding names. Silly labels, because the emotion fear is directly controlled by the Water Element. How stupid to go along and say, 'Come on, pull yourself together. I'll take care of you.' If you had a man that had got a broken arm you wouldn't go up to him and say, 'Oh, hard lines! Now come and play tennis!'

We know that the man with the broken arm cannot scratch his head and surely we should have sufficient understanding to know that the person suffering from that immense fear perhaps cannot go outside and meet people, or perhaps go into confined spaces. Why don't we find out why they cannot do these things?

Now grief. I was relating to you the times when we are likely to grieve at the loss of someone dear to us. One of the senior graduates of the College died, and God, I grieved for two or three days. And I thought, 'Why, why?' Then I realised why, and fine, so now I can talk about him. I couldn't for the first two or three days.

Do you know any people who have gone through this and are still grieving ten, fifteen, twenty years later? 'Ah, my God; if only, if only!' They have not lived from that moment. They look back and their life has been a vacuum. It has been meaningless. It has been nothing. It has just been an existence. They are still grieving, 'Oh, God, if only . . .'

If you have an imbalance on the Metal Element, then, instead of Nature bringing you back to normal, you will stay in grief like the other person stayed in fear. And you will grieve immensely for years and years, until the cause of that emotion of grief is put right by balancing the Lungs and the Colon.

The same happens with the emotion sympathy. You must know the sort of people who come to you, 'Oh, I am ever so pleased you brought me along.' Then they tell you about the last operation, the other operation, and the operation after. And you say, 'Oh you poor little soul.' They are lapping it up. They love you fawning over them. It's imbalance—someone just running everywhere to get as much sympathy as possible. But they can't help it if they have a major imbalance on the Stomach and the Spleen.

This brings us back to love again. Those people you know who have just everything going wrong. They want people to put their arms around them, to love them, to create the Fire.

I was just saying to Patrick and my lovely colleague

Oscar, just while we were having a cup of tea, 'It shows you how barbaric we are. If I had a broken arm, and I was trying to pour out a cup of tea, you would come over and say, 'Hey, let me do that for you J.R.'; and I will say, 'Thank you very much.' If you know my Fire is going out, and I find that I don't love myself I can't love other people, and I say, 'Don't touch me, keep away from me.' So what do we do with such people? Say, 'Oh, leave him alone.' They are the very people we should be going to and giving that Fire so we can help them to get well. Yet what do we do? We can understand the response to a broken arm but we cannot understand the response to a Fire going out.

The way you are going to change—I hope to God—is that when you see you have done this to people, which we all do, I hope you are going to run to them and give them Fire. Give them love, to help to make them well again. And sick people need love more than healthy people. When you are healthy you need it; but, God, when you are sick you need it twice as much. And that is the very thing that we do not give them. Here is a way that we can replenish their Fire and help them recover.

Take anger. I showed you earlier on where the chap comes home and kicks the cat, kicks everybody else, throws the dinner up in the ruddy air, and you can say one or two words wrong and he will hit you in the face. Don't invite him to a party, because if you are having a party, you are not going to have him, because if somebody says something he is going to upset the apple cart. He doesn't want to be like that; but if he has an imbalance on the Element Wood, the emotion of anger becomes imbalanced and he cannot control his anger. But if you balance those two Organs—the Liver and Gall Bladder—that emotion of anger calms down.

I think that it is valuable to know that we are not what we want to be. We are only a manifestation emotionally of what the Organs or the Officials allow us to be. So if you can't love, then look at Fire. If you hate sympathy, or if you want to delve in it all the time, look at the Earth. If you find that you are not grieving, and you have this emptiness in your life, no quality, look at the Metal. If you find you have fear out of all sense of proportion, look at the Water. If you find you cannot control your anger, or someone says, 'Well, I have never lost my temper', which is just as bad as having an excess of temper, look at the Wood.

But, if you have listened to what I said to you earlier, you don't do just that, do you? Because, if you have an anger imbalance, then it may well be coming from the mother. So first thing you have to do is look at the Kidney. If you have a Kidney imbalance, then the first thing that screams will be the child. Therefore the anger will be the first emotion to show. As the disease gets deeper, then the anger will also be accompanied by an excess or a deficiency of fear. So you see, even emotionally we can discern how every Organ in your body is working—but only if we are trained to be able to relate to the emotions.

If the emotions are fitting, then generally it is a sign of health. If they are imbalanced, then it is a sign of disease. That is why we are never, ever, simply physically sick. Mind, body and spirit are one.

If you get a predominant mental imbalance, you don't start doing your exercises and say, 'Well, mentally I feel very depressed, but physically I am fine.' You can't even get your arm up. 'What do you mean, you can't even get your arm up? What's wrong with your arm?' 'Ah, it's too much effort.' See—mind, body and spirit—one. We mustn't listen to one part—to just a symptom that is showing on one part of the body, or the mind, or the spirit, without viewing the cause. Physical diseases can have a mental origin, have a spiritual origin, or can have a physical origin. We must find out which and why.

That, basically, is The Law of Mother/Child. Now we have another Law, The Law of Husband and Wife—which I think we can talk about before you have your roast beef, Yorkshire pudding and your vegetables. Or those of you, of course, who are diet conscious, your hamburger and Coke.

Look at the diagram of the Five Elements again—each time I look at it you know it just amazes me; I just keep saying to myself—the wisdom of these people!

All the Laws are contained in that little drawing. You don't have to *make* them fit; they fit naturally. So, The Law of Husband and Wife. I just want you to sit still on this one, because one or two of you will probably want to go and blow your top. I am talking about 'pre-women's lib'. I'm talking about *natural* laws. Why the hell they have to have a women's lib I do not know! Everybody knows that the man is the head of the family, and that's that! The woman is the neck, and she turns that head whichever direction she wants to!

Everybody also knows that behind every successful man there is a woman. There doesn't have to be anything behind a successful woman; she can do it on her own. Everybody knows that the women are very cunning. They allow the men to put up the fronts and the masculinity and the strength, but it's really they who've got it! They just allow us; they can twist us around their little finger whenever they want to. So why women's lib I don't know. We need a men's lib!

Anyhow, let's just have a look at it, and see how the Chinese saw this five thousand years ago. If you look at the Organs that are on this side of your body, the right hand side, they say that those Organs and pulses belong to the wife. Those of you who are married know that your wife is always right! Those of you who are not yet married will soon find that out! But the Chinese knew that five thousand years ago. So take a leaf from their book and save a lot of torture. It's a natural law that the wife is always right. That's one arm the students never get mixed up with.

And the pulses on the left hand, those are the pulses of the Heart and the Small Intestines, the Liver and the Gall Bladder, and the Bladder and the Kidneys. Those pulses belong to the husband.

The Chinese saw that, if you have a healthy husband and a healthy wife as Nature ordained, the man would be physically stronger. I don't care what you say, that is true; because a man can still run faster, a man can jump higher, than any woman, because he has that physical extra attribute. No women's lib, or anything else, can change the way Nature ordained it to be.

In those days thousands of years ago, of course, the man went out to do the hunting, the shooting and the fishing to provide for the family. The wife stayed at home to play her natural role—to bring up the child; and give strength to the husband, to give him support and love. Without him she would collapse; he would collapse. She feeds the children —that's why I haven't got any breasts. Nature ordained that the woman would feed the child. In that situation, you have a perfect family atmosphere. The father, the husband, does the jobs which Nature ordained—providing—while the mother does the building up and creating the atmosphere of a home—not a house, a home—a place for the children to grow.

You can visualise that, mentally, as a marriage that can last forever. Beautiful. But, supposing the wife has more energy or more power than the husband; she would want to take on his role. She would want to do the running, the shooting and the providing, and, because she is violating a law of Nature, half the fish and the beasts would get away, because she is not fast enough, not strong enough physically, to endure the fight for food. The man would be forced to stay at home to feed the child, and he hasn't even got the equipment. This is a violation of a natural law. Can you see that marriage lasting?

'Ah, ah,' the Chinese said, 'that marriage, that foundation, that life is threatened and will die.' Now you may think that that is dramatic; but it's true. Because another thing we can do in traditional Chinese medicine is, when we make a correct diagnosis, in many cases we will find within a patient there is a Husband/Wife imbalance. That means that we have the situation I have just described going on inside. We have the wife part trying to violate the law of Nature by taking the male role, and there is destruction. Do you know what that means? When we are able to diagnose that, the patient is definitely going to die. Not might. Not perhaps. But *will* definitely die. The Chinese knew in their wisdom that as the family will perish so will the family *within* perish. And it could be that you would die in a period of anything up to six months; certainly no longer.

So here again is another joyous thing that we are able to do—by following natural laws. If we do discern and detect the Husband/Wife imbalance within a patient, with the grace of God, we are able to correct that imbalance and give back the superior energy to the husband, put the wife back in her role, and that patient will then live for their normal life expectancy.

If there is any greater joy in this world I want to know what it is! To think that perhaps in my short life, and I'm only twenty (but I do lie!), I have probably corrected as many as three or four hundred Husband/Wife imbalances. That means, through the grace of God, and through this beautiful system of medicine, people are still alive today who otherwise would have died. What a joyous feeling it is. And all of it is made possible just by understanding Nature and understanding natural law.

So a Husband/Wife imbalance shows us the severity

of disease and how long the patient has got on the face of this earth.

You see, it doesn't always happen that a person dies by a natural progression of illness. You must have known cases where someone says, 'Hey, John Smith died last week.' 'What, last week?' 'God, he was in the pub the night before. He looked as healthy as could be.' He just doesn't die suddenly like that. The odds are that he had a Husband/Wife imbalance and, as soon as it breaks through at a certain stage, immediately there is a complete break, a pull away of life, and he dies. Another reason this system of medicine must be encouraged and practised in the Western world is because we can save thousands and thousands of unnecessary deaths by being able to discern a Husband/Wife imbalance. Violation of natural law. Neither man nor woman can violate Nature, without paying for it.

So there are two very simple Laws—The Law of Mother/Child which anyone can understand, And The Law of Husband/Wife, which is rather frightening. But it is very encouraging that if you are able to rebalance the energy, someone is going to live who would otherwise die.

There is one way too that we can detect impending death. Again, you may not be able to detect it by a progression of illness. All the people who die suddenly must always die of Aggressive Energy or Husband/Wife imbalance. You can't suddenly die any other way. Every person, who dies suddenly, dies of one of those two things. If you are permeated with Aggressive Energy, and we can remove it, you will live a normal life expectancy. If we don't you will die within the space of three, four, five months. Here again is another frightening yet exciting aspect—that here you have the ability to assist Nature and thus preserve life, which is a very, very joyous thing to do.

How long do you want for lunch? Ten minutes? This is something I want you to think about. If I said we are not going to have lunch, there would be a certain amount of disquiet, and you would be saying, 'Now, wait a minute! I haven't had anything to eat since breakfast.' So now you want to rush to your mother again. I mean, you were at your mother's breast at breakfast time, I hope; or you will be tomorrow, after I have told you something about the Chinese Clock. But now you are wanting to dash to your mother again. You want to go wherever you are going to, and you are going to eat. And you are going to come back this afternoon, and you are going to be stuffed, and you are going to be tired, and half of you are going to go to sleep.

'Oh, it's so important that I have something to eat.' Now, what I would like some of you to do is to go out and say, 'Hey, Mum, I had a breastful this morning.' Instead, go out and take in some of the air that your Father provides, because, you know, you can go ten days without food and you won't die, but you can't go four minutes without air. You do not live on food alone. If you go out and get in contact with your Father and breathe deeply and re-energise your vital Qi energy, and you come back in here this afternoon, you will be ready to listen. Take your choice. The canteen will probably crucify me for reducing their profits; so how about a compromise? Go out and get some fresh air first and, when you come back, you will feel more like eating. How long? Three quarters of an hour, plenty? An hour? What do you want? It's just gone one quarter to one; shall we kick off at quarter to two?

Afternoon

My God, gluttons for punishment!

What I want to do this afternoon is to me a fun thing. I think you will get more from this than anything else we have discovered or discussed so far. I do feel I should say to you that, when discussing laws like The Law of Mother/Child, Husband/Wife, I don't want you to think that's the Law in its entirety. Obviously I can't convey to you in the space of a few hours what takes me six or seven years to convey to my graduates.

I'm just giving you enough so that you get a basic understanding. We can talk about The Law of Mother/Child for three whole days and still not exhaust it. I mean, I don't want to blind you by talking beyond your level—although I understand you have no level, you are already right up there! I'm trying to keep friendly with Oscar, you see!

What we are going to do now is discuss one of the other Laws, and this is The Law of Midday/Midnight. We will see again how we make ourselves sick, again by violating the laws of Nature.

It wouldn't surprise me if some of you don't understand, or even know, that you have a clock of your own. You have. When you were born, Nature built a clock in you so that you could listen to the clock and look at the clock and learn a lot of information from it. Now we decide, 'Hell, who wants a Nature's clock? Let's have one of these mechanical clocks.' Then what we do is govern our lives by this thing.

This thing (wrist watch) causes as much disease as anything else. I give you an instance. There was a certain beautiful young lady whom I was passionately in love with. She was obviously sick because she was in love with me too. We agreed that we would meet at half-past-ten, and our hearts were light and bounding and thinking what was going to happen at half-past-ten. Unfortunately I got delayed, and she was there at half-past-ten and I arrived at about a-quarter-to-eleven. As soon as I said, 'Hello darling', she said, 'Where the hell have you been? I have been here for fifteen minutes, and it's raining and I'm freezing cold. I'm not going with you now!' Just because that clock hand was that little bit further on than when we had agreed to meet. I haven't got to be there at ten o'clock; I have got to be there at half-past. This thing is dictating our lives!

Now I know we have got to pay some respect to it. But we want balance and moderation, and combine them with our own internal clock.

Every Organ in your body has a two hour period of maximum capacity. This means that for two hours only each Organ in turn has more energy, is more dynamic, than at any other time during the day.

You may say, 'Hey, so what? What does that tell me?' Well, you know that many people, when they are not well, find the day sort of goes like this. You get up in the morning and you say to your loved one, 'Hello darling, how are you?' 'Ugh!' What have we got for breakfast, darling?' 'Ugh, don't talk to me. I'm not alive yet.' Then round about twelve o'clock she starts coming into the land of the living and says, 'Well, how are you?' There's half the day gone!

And you get the others who get up in the morning,

and they're off like a lark. And then, round about twelve o'clock, you say, 'How are you doing?' 'Ah, not now, I'm exhausted.' Round about midday and, 'I have got no energy.'

Different times of the day. Some people don't really start to come alive in the morning, that's the worst part of the day. Some people get up O.K., and then, just after lunch, they flop. Other people go on and, round about night time, they just disintegrate. Others don't come alive until night time. You know, they are zombies all day and round about ten o'clock, 'Come on, let's get going.' And yet all day you couldn't speak to them.

Seriously, I mean very seriously, here's a good little exercise to do to give you a sense of proportion. *You have never had a day like today.* There will never be another Sunday like this in the rest of your life. It's the only one, and you only go through it once. To hell! Let's live it. Let's learn something. Let's love somebody. Let's grow from it. You know? You need to use every minute of this day. I mean, to be out of the day for half of it; you might just as well be dead! What's the use of getting up every day and half the day is of no use. If you live to be sixty, really you have only lived to be thirty. You have wasted the other thirty years.

If you are reasonably balanced in body, mind and spirit, then, sure, you have your little ups and downs during the day, but by and large you go to bed and say, 'Hey, you know, that was good! A bit of negativity but by and large that was a great day! Wow, we have got another one tomorrow.' How many of us say, 'Well, tomorrow I'll . . . tomorrow I'll . . .' And tomorrow never comes. By the time it does come, you are ruddy dead!

Instead of looking at this watch all the time, look at your body-clock. If this imbalance is happening to you during the day, at a certain time during the day, that's a distress signal from the body saying, 'Hey, something's going wrong!'

Take the twelve Organs of the body. Divide a circle into twelve equal parts. I am an absolute expert at doing this; mind you, if I don't get twelve, I get fourteen, and it somehow doesn't seem to work out! So I hope there are twelve there. Yes.

Here then we have twelve parts of the twenty-four hours of the day, and twelve Organs.

Between 11.00 o'clock at night and 1.00 o'clock in the morning your Gall-Bladder has the maximum peak of activity. That much more energy than at any other time during the day and night. From 1.00 o'clock in the morning until 3.00 o'clock in the morning your Liver takes over and has its maximum period of activity.

From 3.00 o'clock in the morning until 5.00 o'clock in the morning your Lungs have the maximum period of activity; 5.00 until 7.00 it is your Colon; 7.00 till 9.00 it is your Stomach. So we go round the circle. Spleen is 9.00 to 11.00, Heart is 11.00 o'clock in the morning until 1.00 o'clock in the afternoon, the Small Intestines 1.00 o'clock in the afternoon until 3.00 o'clock, the Bladder from 3.00 o'clock until 5.00, the Kidney from 5.00 to 7.00, Circulation-Sex—we are going to discuss that later—is from 7.00 until 9.00, and the Three Heater is from 9.00 until 11.00.

Two hours during the day and night when each one of the Organs has much more energy than at any other time. If we were to respect that, and pay some credence to it, we would be very much healthier.

Look for example at the Colon meridian. The Colon has that much more energy from 5.00 o'clock to 7.00 o'clock in the morning than at any other time during the twenty-four hours. Emptying your bowels, going to the toilet and defecating, is very important. We recognise that; we need to take away the pollution and poison from the body. Otherwise, if we leave it in the body then all of that evil smelling waste matter starts to pollute the blood, and the

The Chinese Clock

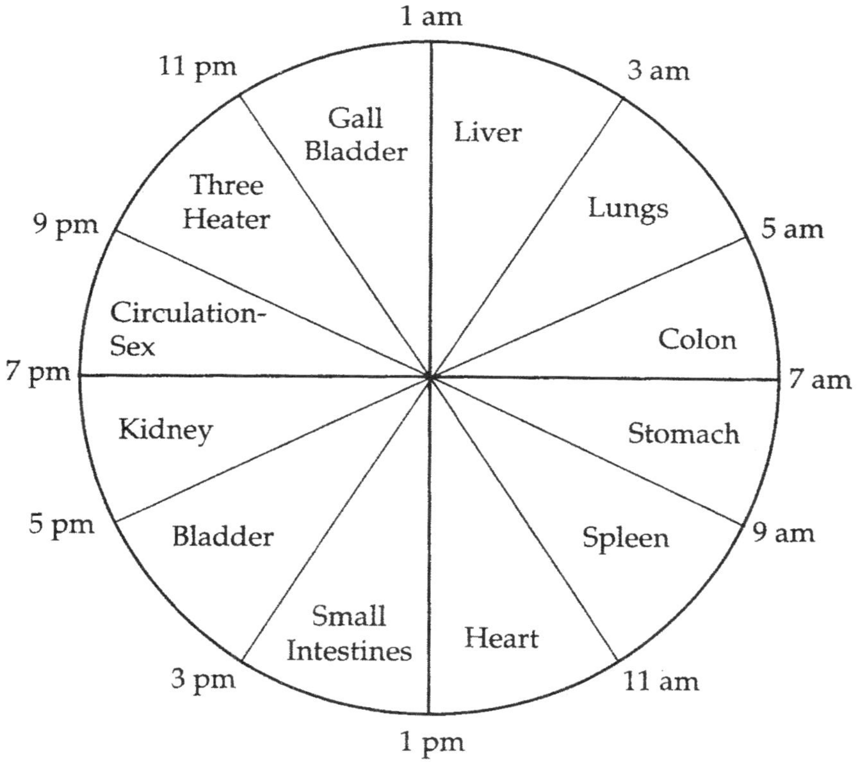

whole system becomes polluted and dirty. To keep our bodies clean we need to take away the waste matter. That is how we see it in the West; but, again, the wisdom of the Chinese shows that you don't just defecate physically. Think of the filth and the pollution that comes into the mind each day. We need also to get rid of that. If your mind gets constipated and bogged up with filth, then imagine how your whole life style is going to change.

People do evil, filthy, dirty, degrading things. Nobody who is reasonably healthy in body, mind and spirit would do them. But if the mind is polluted, there is no way that you can do anything about it. So the mind also needs the Official, the appropriate Organ, to discard the filth, the negativity, the hostility, the anger. All of that needs to be evacuated so that, when you start the day, you start with a clean mind and a clean body. If not, then that day is wasted, because your mind is constipated.

You have heard people say, 'I'm not interested; oh, get out of the way.' 'Don't believe that; that's a load of filth; that's a load of rubbish; keep out of it!' They don't want to join in, they won't listen, they won't hear, they won't want to discuss anything because their mind is so full. Just as, when you are really badly constipated, if someone says, 'Come on, let's go and have a nice meal' you'd say, 'Oh, God, no! I feel so . . . ugh! No I don't want to.' If any more were put in, it's only going to be polluted, and not do your body any good at all.

So, too, there is a great need to cleanse the spirit. When you go to the toilet in the morning, don't think that you just take away body waste. This Organ, this Official, also controls the waste of the mind and the waste of the spirit. It is most important, when you start the day, that you get all of the filth, the toxins out of the body, mind and spirit. Then you are receptive, and you are clean to enjoy all the things that are available.

Twenty three percent of the population of this country, and my own country, suffer from constipation, chronic constipation—you can tell that by the vast amount of laxatives that are taken, and bran, and all the other things, trying to force this waste matter out. Heaven forbid! You shouldn't force it; it's a natural function. If they went to the toilet for one month, between the hours of 5.00 and 7.00, when this organ has that much more activity, I would gamble that ninety percent of the world's constipation problems would be solved.

But that's too easy! People don't want to get up at five o'clock in the morning and go to the toilet. 'Oh, hell, I'll have another hour in bed and take a laxative.' Small wonder there is sickness. Or they get up and say, 'Oh, I haven't got time to go to the toilet. I will go later on.' And then they go to work, and round about three o'clock they say, 'Oh, my God, I haven't been to the toilet.' They sit there, go black in the face, and nothing happens! Oh, my God, I'm constipated.'

All the Organs in your body—which the Chinese call Officials, not Organs—work in exactly the same way. This particular Official, the Colon, can virtually eliminate your spirit, if you allow it, during its maximum natural period. That's why Nature gave these particular Organs their turn in a natural cycle.

I hope you are going to listen to this because, not only is it necessary to have a clean body, but it's imperative to have a clean mind. Otherwise you are cutting out so many things that can come in new and fresh each day. There is so much sickness of the mind. You can start calling it 'schizo', or some such silly label. But the only way you can eradicate mental pollution is by eliminating it when you go to the toilet.

Some people don't like talking about defecation. To hell with that! It's a beautiful subject to talk about. I'm ever so pleased I do it. But I will tell you this. If you change the time you open your bowels, and you go in the morning, between five and seven, I will promise you that you will pass twice as much waste matter after a month than you have previously been passing.

Many feel they have been to the toilet if they pass one or two stools; but they leave the other two or three stools inside them. I gamble, if you are passing on average a couple of stools, in the space of a month of going to the toilet between five and seven o'clock in the morning, you will pass three or four. Your body and mind will be much cleaner as a result; and so will your spirit.

So, take a lesson. Tomorrow morning round about five o'clock, I want to hear about a hundred and forty chains going at the same time! A massive flush! Then I shall know indeed that today has been worthwhile!

Seriously, seriously, I really want you to do it. So much increase of the natural joy and beauty you could share. The learning experience of every day is negated if your mind is full. Be receptive, so that you can take in as much as possible all day long.

You get up and bathe yourself; you take the physical waste and dirt away from your physical body. But I suggest you leave that on, and go to the toilet instead! It is much more important to clean the inside than it is to clean the outside. Obviously, it is better to clean both; but the importance is not the shower, the real importance is the toilet. I don't mind you going to work saying, 'I haven't got time to have a shower.' But I do mind you going to work unclean in mind and spirit.

Now, let's start to look and see how further barbaric we get! From seven o'clock to nine o'clock in the morning the Stomach Official contains that much more energy than at any other time during the day. This means that, at that time, your Stomach could virtually digest a ruddy nail! Ready to go, and whatever you send down it will just devour it.

That's how Nature ordained it should be; not man, *Nature*. Why shouldn't we listen to Nature? We know we cannot improve upon it; but we say, 'Of course we can improve on Nature.' So the average person gets up in the morning, and you say to him or her, 'What did you have for breakfast?' 'Well, I had half a piece of toast.' So, there they are—body, mind and spirit—going off with an almost empty tank. Then they say, 'Oh, God, I am tired! . . . Oh, I have got no energy . . . Oh dear, my back does hurt.' Trying to drive this body along without fuel. You wouldn't do that with your motor car!

Come the end of the day, and you have done all your work with virtually no fuel. Marvellous how Nature lets you do it. Nothing else would let you do it. You do it, but Nature is compassionate. It knows we are a bunch of ruddy idiots and it's compassionate. Otherwise we would all be dead by the time we were twelve. Then, we turn round and say, 'Who do I really love?' Who needs friends when we treat ourselves like this?

I say, 'I love you. Would you come out to dinner with me tonight?' 'Yes please; oh, yes.' What time shall we eat?' 'Round about seven o'clock to nine.' Now, that's just the time when this Stomach Official is at its maximum period of rest! But we say, 'Hey, come on now! How about steak?' 'Yes please.' Send it down! 'And how about some chips and a hamburger, and some French fries? And how about some gateau? Would you like a coffee?' 'No, I will have two coffees.' 'Want some more gateau, and have some sweet as well?' 'Hope you enjoyed your meal!' You go back to bed, and say, 'I hope you can ruddy well sleep as well!' Because here's this Stomach Official, ready to devour anything in the morning, and you say, 'Well, there's a cornflake, keep quiet.' And then—when all the energy has been expended, and he's thinking, 'Oh my, I am exhausted', and he's starting to rest—you say, 'Come on! Now start digesting this dinner.'

We are crazy! Small wonder you can't sleep. You are filling up during the night, and you have a headache in the morning, and no vitality. Stark raving mad! Now, if you really love somebody, say, 'Hey, I love you. Would you like to come round to have breakfast with me?' 'Breakfast?' 'Yes, come on, let's have breakfast.' And then, whatever you eat is not only fueling you to go on during the day, but you could virtually, as I say, eat nails and they would be digested. You certainly can't digest food at the minimum energy period of the stomach.

So, there are two things you have got to learn for the preservation of health. You have to strive towards health *yourself*, by obeying natural laws. One is, you empty your bowels; you get rid of the pollution and the filth of the body and the mind and the spirit. Then you bring in the vital essence provided by your Mother so that it can be digested and so that energy is there for you to utilise during the course of the day. Your main meal should be your breakfast.

I am not going to ask how many of you make breakfast your main meal because it will be very embarrassing! But I hope, if ever I do come back, I will say, 'What's your main meal?' and you'll reply, 'Breakfast, after we have been to the toilet.' Then I am sure we will have a healthier nation!

It is small wonder that we get sickness. The Chinese would have said, 'Who are these so called civilised barbaric idiots?' So, if you want to maintain health, just follow these two things, and, my God, I gamble that you will have much more vitality, much more energy, much more drive. And you will be a little lighter.

You don't have to gorge yourself, but really tank up in the morning. Don't just fill your car, fill your body. If we paid half as much respect to our body, mind and spirit as we do to our cars, we wouldn't know what to do with the doctors. They would have nothing to do. We would suffer from a health epidemic; instead we are hell bent on making ourselves sick by violating natural laws.

We say, 'What time is lunch?' 'Well, it's one o'clock.' Who the hell wants to eat at one o'clock? 'I'm not hungry.' 'Well, it's one o'clock. I have got your lunch ready.' 'Oh, all right; I'll eat it.' It doesn't do you any good at all. You can't assimilate it, and you can't digest it.

So, two things before we leave food. One is, basically, eat when you are hungry. If you are not hungry, don't eat. A very simple rule. How many times have you sat down and eaten something when you didn't really want it? The answer is, don't eat it. You make sure you have your main meal in the morning.

The second is very, very important, and it's a very simple thing. When you are eating your food, during this maximum time in the morning, always remember a little golden rule my father used to tell me—drink your food and eat your drinks. That means chew your food until it is almost like a liquid. Don't swallow great lumps of stuff leaving it for the Stomach Official to churn up. You do the churning up with the equipment up here in your mouth before you send it down. And if you are drinking something, take wisdom from little babies—no baby will just drink. The baby mixes drink with his own saliva, thus getting total assimilation of all necessary things—from both food and the drink. For what does a baby do if he is not given time to do this? He vomits it all back again. So it is very important to mix your drink with your saliva. This is one of the reasons it is there.

Now I don't suppose that inspires you very much, although it is the way that you can make yourself healthier. But you are not going to do it, because it's too easy. Most people want somebody else to make them well. But I strongly suggest you start taking the responsibility of the doctor. It is your responsibility; the doctor is only there to help you when Nature breaks down.

Now let's have a look at this Clock again and see how it can tell us so many things. Let us suppose that you have hyperfunctioning on the Gall Bladder. Remember the balance I was talking about? So here we have the Gall Bladder with too much energy. Too much activity wasting away.

Malfunction of the Gall Bladder can give anything up to a hundred symptoms. One can be left-sided or right-sided migraine. Another can be disturbed vision; another can be nausea, vomiting. Other ones can be pain in the hip or the inability to articulate freely the joints in your body. A multiplicity of symptoms can be caused by malfunction of the Gall Bladder.

If it is hyperfunctioning, too much energy, you can get any of these symptoms. Then, between eleven o'clock and one o'clock at night, it hyperfunctions even more. So the symptoms are exacerbated, and become much worse. There are certain people whom you can ask, 'Is there a particular time of day when you feel better or worse?' And every sick person can tell you one time of the day when they are better or worse. From their own internal clocks they can at least zone in to which Organ is crying out for help.

We can see how we are all so very different. There is no point in the person suffering from hyperfunction of the Gall Bladder going to bed at 11.00 o'clock at night, because that is when it comes to the maximum period of activity and exacerbates the symptoms. That person is going to toss and turn; and they will read; and they will say, 'I can't sleep until so and so . . .' They don't fall off to sleep until one o'clock—until this maximum hyperactivity has passed by.

What have we learnt from that? That if you find when you go to bed that you are tossing and turning for a period of time, then go to bed an hour earlier. It could well be that you will be into sleep before this hyperfunctioning can disturb you; on the other hand, if it is excessive, it may still do so.

This is particularly so with the Liver. A vast number of people go to bed and wake up any time between one and three; they could set their alarm clocks by it. They say, 'Every morning I go down, have a cigarette, have a cup of tea, go to the toilet, walk round, read for a bit, and then I go back to bed and finally fall off to sleep.' Other people wake up at five o'clock in the morning. They say, 'I can't go back to sleep again after that.' These are all distress signals coming from their internal clocks telling them that something is wrong. So why don't they listen to them?

So . . . very, very important. If you find that you suddenly have a great dip during any time of the day then, very often, you can align this to a particular Organ.

On the other hand, you may get a situation where a person is in pain and has, say—to use a silly label—arthritis. The cause of this, shall we say, is hypofunctioning of the Bladder. That means too little energy. Therefore the body (and the mind and the spirit) is struggling to motivate itself in the morning. Then, round about that time in the afternoon when Nature gives it its extra hyperfunctioning, that plus virtually wipes out the minus, and many patients will say, 'About three o'clock or five o'clock in the afternoon, I feel, you know, oh, much better. And then it comes back again.'

The Chinese Clock, the person's own internal clock, gives all that very valid information. It's valuable diagnostically. For instance, you can't come to life in the morning if you have got hyperfunctioning of the Stomach or the Spleen. By the time you wake up, you have got this hyperfunctioning, so you feel really right out of it, and don't come back into circulation again until the Organ has passed through its time period.

This hyperfunctioning is why you obliterate various parts of the day, where you just go to pieces, or you're not with it, or you get hyperactive. All this is governed by your own internal clock. So you need to look at this. It's well worth your time trying to remember the various hours that are associated with your own internal organs. Not only listen to what they are trying to tell you, but also try to follow them, particularly, as I say, in the discipline of elimination in the morning and the taking in of food.

Western medicine ties up with this Chinese Clock in that the highest incidence of cardiac failures occur between the hours of 11.00 o'clock and 1.00 o'clock in the day. If the patient lives through that period, then the highest death rate comes between 11.00 o'clock and 1.00 o'clock at night. The first is the maximum time of the Heart and the second the minimum time of the Heart. That is recognised in Western medicine, yet the Chinese had it all planned out five thousand years ago.

So that's just a very basic description of The Law of Midday/Midnight, or the Chinese Clock, or your own internal clock. Just see how it can explain many phenomena. It is why you do this up-and-downing. If you can help to level this out, then it makes life much more enjoyable.

Nature ordained that we live in contact with our Mother. This is why we are always in contact with the earth. We are like little children; we can never leave our Mother Earth—except, that is when you go in an aeroplane.

When I boarded the plane at Heathrow to come over here, I was full of the joys of spring and thought, 'Hallelujah, I am going to have seven hours with no phone calls, no patients, no anxiety, no worry. Seven hours to myself. Eureka!' And I sat there on the plane and I read, and I have not been able to do that for ages. I listened to some music. I saw a funny movie. I bought my own food. And I got off the plane, and there was Richard waiting. He said, 'Hello J.R.' and I said, 'Hello Richard.' Blimey! I was virtually spaced-out! That was because I violated a natural law, by leaving Mother Earth.

My Chinese internal clock couldn't adjust. My internal clock said to me, 'Hey, it's midnight.' But my watch, when I adjusted it here, said, 'No, it ain't you know; it's seven o'clock.' So my internal clock was trying to fight with this thing, and they were totally at odds. Plus the fact that I had left the earth. That's why you get jet-lag; not for any other reason at all. Violation of a natural law, and an interference with the internal clock.

If you are reasonably healthy, your internal clock can balance within about a day. If you are not healthy it can be ten to twelve days before it catches up. But, for a time, you are still semi spaced-out and jet-lagged, not knowing whether to go to the toilet, have breakfast, have dinner or go to bed.

Yet five thousand years ago they could have told us the price we have to pay if we violate a natural law by travelling in an aeroplane. And the longer you are away from Mother Earth, the more severe becomes the jet-lag, and the longer it takes for your internal clock to readjust. If you want to go anywhere, walk; and at least you will get there healthy!

I find this very valuable. Any person can get in tune with their own body clock. So, if you find you are having a very difficult time during the day, that is another distress signal from Nature saying, 'Hey, let's get this seen to.'

Now we come to the last law—The Law of Cure.

Every disease has to follow a Law of Cure, if you are going to be cured. It is mind-blowing that you are cured *according to natural law*.

We can tell by observing this law whether our patients are going to be cured if we must use that word, and I hate using it—or whether we can only palliate, or whether we can only get so far and no further. We don't have to guess and hope they will get better. We know whether they will or not, according to this law.

The Law of Cure states—and this is for the benefit of those of you who are patients and do not know this—that the disease has to come from within to the outside; from above to below; and it will disappear in the reverse order from which it came.

This is why we want to know all of your case history. You may well come to us, shall we say, with some mental disorder, or with migraine, whatever it may be. And your practitioner tries to ask all of the previous diseases that you have had. The classic, simple case to explain why he does this is that of asthma, or bronchial emphysema. The patient says, 'Well, when I was about twelve I had very, very bad acne. Then when I was about nine, I remember I had the ague, and my mother was worried to death about this.'

Now, if we are going to cure this patient of asthma, as we are cleaning from within to outside, the original skin disease must reappear. Although he may not have had it for ten years, it may only reappear for only one day, it may only reappear for one hour, it may reappear for one year. But he need not worry over it; for once it has reappeared it will go for ever.

We need to know this law because many patients come and say, 'Look, I came for my asthma, and now my skin disease has come back, and I haven't had that since I was ten.' Wonderful! It means that you have cleansed the person right out back to the age when they were ten. The first symptoms will naturally come out in reverse with the furtherance of the treatment.

Again it is important to know this law with, say, arthritic people who say, 'You know, my head's better, my neck's better, but my hands have never been worse! I'd rather stop the treatment. I mean, I can't even pick things up now.' Beautiful! It has to come from above to below. Then the patient can realise why the practitioner doesn't get upset if the lower extremities become worse than they have ever been; because that is the natural course the cure follows.

But, if the patient turns round and says, 'My hands are marvellous, but my shoulder's worse,' then we know something's wrong. This is a violation of The Law of Cure.

So we have to see that the disease is being cured in the natural way. The most joyous words we ever want to hear from a patient is when they come and we say, 'How are you?' are 'Oh, gosh, this pain really is awful doctor!' We can say, 'O.K. my love, don't worry. We are doing all we can.' 'But I feel better inside.' Bang! We know from that word onwards, the law is being followed. Because, although the pain may be one year, two years—I don't know how long it is before it will go, and go for ever—the first sign has to be that the patient feels better inside. Then we know we are following The Law of Cure.

However, it is, again, a little more complicated than that. What does sometimes happen is that a physical disease, when it reappears, may only reappear on a mental level; it doesn't have to reappear on a physical level. That, again, is to show you why we ask so many questions, so that, as you are getting better, we make sure it is following The Law of Cure. If it isn't, then you will seem to get better and then, suddenly, go right back to where you were—which is a total waste of time.

So we know whether cure is going to be effective and whether it is following the natural path.

The five basic laws—The Law of the Five Elements, The Law of Mother/Child, The Law of Midday/Midnight, The Law of Husband/Wife and The Law of Cure. Each one of these you can study in depth for a whole year and not scratch the surface. But I hope I have given you a very rough appreciation of them.

I would like now to go on to Functions, because in every Western Science school they teach all about the heart and the small intestines and the bladder and the liver and the kidneys and so on, and sometimes I am amazed at the skill of a Western physician who, let's face it, does cure and does help so many people. But how they do it without acknowledging the two most important functions in the body just blows my mind; I just don't know how they do it!

Let's have a look at the first function which is Circulation-Sex. It is so called because that is what it is primarily responsible for. It is responsible for the arterial and the venous blood. Many of you may have thought that was the responsibility of the Heart, but it isn't. It is controlled by Circulation-Sex.

The second part is called Sex because this function governs all internal and external sexual secretions. I want you to remember too that it belongs to the Element Fire. We can all realise that blood is associated with fire and red and warmth, so that we may get a patient come with very cold hands, very cold feet, and that can be—but not always—a distress signal from Circulation-Sex. It is not functioning correctly because it can't get the blood down to the extremities, or it can't hasten the return, and you know what happens if you have malfunction in venous return: varicose veins and haemorrhoids. You know what happens too if you have a major malfunction of Circulation-Sex. You become impotent or frigid; or if it is hyperfunctioning, you become hypersexed. Those vital features of your arterial blood which goes to every cell in your body, and of your venous blood which is responsible for coming back to cleanse and reoxygenate the internal and external sexual secretions, are totally governed by this function. It's mind blowing!

You see many unfortunate people with major sexual disorders. This is indeed a tragedy because, normally, man and woman were designed by Nature to come together for the procreation of children. It is the most meaningful thing in the world. I don't mean getting into bed with people;

that is a physical act of love. But when a man really loves a woman, and a woman really loves a man, then they come together as Nature ordained, and the two then become one. The love is physical, mental and spiritual, and at the time of lovemaking and the climax you get a spiritual fusion. That's why you often hear even atheists say, 'God!' For that moment, there are three of you. You, her and God. And there is no time.

That is about the most joyous beautiful experience. You say, 'How long did it last? Was it a minute, was it a lifetime, was it ten lifetimes?' The joy and the beauty in that is absolutely indescribable. That's how Nature ordained it should be. How many people get married, how many people love each other, and have never ever experienced anything like it? If you have a malfunction in Circulation-Sex, that is beyond you. You cannot reach that. It becomes physically satisfying, mentally alright, but who is going to accept that instead of what I have just described?

You may find that a man and woman may love each other most sincerely. Then, suddenly, he finds that he can't get an erection. That part of their marriage is threatened. There is no way they can share those moments. God, who the hell wants to live if you can't share those moments? I mean, that is the quality of life. That's how Nature ordained things should be. You've got a barren marriage, and then what's going to happen to the woman? The woman can become frigid. What's going to happen to the man? He's going to turn to drink. He's going to smoke excessively. He's going to go somewhere else.

All these millions of complications can cause disease and depression, because this vital essence that Nature ordained we should share is void. Circulation-Sex governs it. That is why it is so heartbreaking when people have these marital problems of not being able to teach this in orthodox medical schools. This is where half your 'schizos' come from. This is where a person goes out of their mind.

We can control this through the Circulation-Sex meridian. We can balance the energy that controls not only the physical sexual organs—don't think that sexual organs are only physical, they are not; they are also mental; they are also spiritual. The fulfilment I have described to you can basically only come about if Circulation-Sex is pretty much in balance.

Many of the early symptoms may just simply be cold hands and cold feet. But if you let that go on and on, then the disease manifests at a deeper level; then you start to get your sexual problem. Imbalances. So how joyous is it that we can bring that back into many people's lives by being able to treat on this particular meridian.

The Chinese didn't use the words 'heart,' 'small intestines,' 'liver' and 'gall bladder.' They didn't know what the hell they were! And why I think I like the system of medicine so much is because it is so child-like; and I love being a child.

I remember, when I was first studying Western medicine, I think I was a bit of an authority on lungs. This is because my father showed me a book, and in this book were two little men, and they were using bellows, and immediately I realised what they were doing. And I thought, 'Hey, that's pretty good.' When I had tutors teaching me anatomy and physiology, nobody made so much influence on my mind. Whatever words they used, there was still this little picture.

Now the Chinese depicted each Organ in your body as being an Official. That means a little man if you like. Oh, that may sound idiotic, sound child-like, but you can't beat the wisdom of children! And they saw that each Official had a specific job to do in the body, and that the organ itself is really only one minor part of the total picture.

So, for example, the Official of Circulation-Sex is

really called the Heart Protector. (The full term, of course, is not just 'heart'; the Heart is called the Supreme Controller.) They saw this Supreme Controller as a man, as a God, as a King, as an Emperor; the one with authority to control the other eleven Officials. They knew full well all the trials and tribulations that the eleven Organs have—the frustrations, the tensions, the anxieties, the malfunctions. All the Officials turn to the King and say, 'Please help me, please help me, please help me!' Now he's trying to co-ordinate the body, mind and spirit, and each of the other eleven Officials, and he's got one terrible, enormous task. And if everybody keeps coming to him they will destroy him. So he has a protector; and Circulation-Sex is called the Protector of the Supreme Controller.

It is like a wall around the King. So, if the King has this wall around him to protect him from insults and injuries that would be hurled at him, then he can spend all of his energies in controlling, caring, and loving his people.

If the defence mechanism—the Circulation-Sex, the Supreme Controller's Protector—is sick, that leaves the Heart totally vulnerable. The Heart or Supreme Controller was not designed to take insults and injuries. It has to be protected.

So, here you will find too, that, as with marital affairs and with relationships, many people can get devastated by a love 'disease.' Other people can get over it pretty easily. If you have a good Heart Protector then, basically, this major hurt to the Heart doesn't really get to the Heart. It's caught by the Heart Protector, and only a very little of it infiltrates into the Heart.

But if the Supreme Controller is weak, Circulation-Sex is weak, and the Heart is vulnerable. How many times have you heard people say, I will never get over that; he broke my heart.' He did *break* her heart; or she did *break* his heart; and they will never be the same again. And they will say, 'I can't deal with it, I can't cope. I don't want another relationship. I don't want to be hurt like that again. There's no way I can go through that again.' Of course they can't!

If you cannot build up a defence around your Heart, then you can't go out and have another go. This is why a lot of people who have had one bad relationship spend the rest of their lives not going into another. How horrible! If we could just build up the protection of the Heart then we could then go into another relationship without having such a major scar. The Protector has an invaluable function. The most important thing about it is—as you can see how much it is to do with blood and relationships—that this function has more control over love and joy and laughter and real beauty than even the Heart itself.

So we find with many people that there is no sunshine in their lives. There is no joy, there is no laughter. It's just purgatory going on from day to day. Mentally, physically, spiritually there is no love, there is no warmth, there is no anything. You can bring all that back to someone if you reinforce the Circulation-Sex function. You just think of the thousands of people who are in this horrible situation who can be brought back into a meaningful life by controlling Circulation-Sex. Why on earth they don't teach it in orthodox medical schools I have no idea!

You may wonder at times, when you see things in the newspaper about someone doing something depraved and filthy to a little child or to a woman. No one in their right mind would ever do that unless they were sick. But if you are hyperfunctioning on this particular function, your whole sexual control goes almost stark raving mad. That's why people do it. And if we were able to calm them down, to bring them to normal, they would be as nauseated at the thought of what they have done as we are when we read about it.

Now we see how people do this through sickness. We see how people hurt each other through sickness, and we see how people ostracise each other through sickness. If we can realise that, then we can understand better why people do things, and then we can lend ourselves to support them.

But what we are doing today in this century is putting these sick people into institutions. We are putting them into prisons. We are condemning them to their sickness of the mind or the spirit, and that really isn't a way to treat our own brothers and sisters.

True, we may need to put them in there for safety's sake; but what we also need to do is to find out why they do these things. They do these things through sickness of the mind and the body which, with the aid of this system of medicine, we are able to help to put right.

The Three Heater is another function which you can understand very easily—particularly those poor, dear, beautiful, young ladies who go through 'the change.' If you notice, I have a tremendous empathy or love or affection for ladies. I think they are all beautiful, and that is basically because my heart bleeds for them. I mean, the average young girl can go to the physician and say, 'Doctor, I have got this awful pain in my tummy and I don't feel at all well.' The child is round about twelve. And the doctor says, 'Well, you will be O.K. when you have your periods.' The child goes away and then the periods start. She goes to the doctor and says, 'Oh doctor, you know, I am getting these pains here, and I just don't feel well at all.' 'Oh, well, you will be O.K. when you have had a baby.' Later, she has a baby, two babies, and goes back to her doctor and says, 'Doctor, I don't feel well.' And he says, 'Oh, gosh, I shouldn't think so, at your age.'

So, you know, the poor women can't win. They are condemned for a whole lifetime.

Now let's look at the Three Heater. I'll give you a simple analogy here. You really are beautiful people—I really have enjoyed today! Sorry I have got to go to

Maryland tomorrow; but I shall love being in Maryland tomorrow; there are some beautiful people there too!

Now, you are sitting in this room and you are listening to what it is I am trying to share with you. Let us imagine that the temperature of the room suddenly dropped to freezing point. There is nothing wrong with you mentally, physically or spiritually. You are fine; you are healthy people. I have never seen such a healthy bunch of people! So, suddenly the room goes down to freezing point. All O.K.; and then, oh my God, awful; and then you are not listening. I mean, you can't hear a word I am saying. You are suddenly so involved in yourself. Yet there's nothing wrong with you organically, mentally or spiritually. But, because the temperature in which you are functioning drops, you cease to function. You can't hear; you are not interested; you don't write; all you are concerned with is, 'God, I'm ruddy cold! Let's get out of here! Let's put an overcoat on, or let's do something.' On the other hand, you could turn round and bring the temperature of the room up to about 90° and you think, 'God, phew . . . !' Again, you won't listen, you won't be able to hear. So, really, you only function effectively if you are functioning in the right temperature externally. Isn't that true?

Every one of the twelve Organs and twelve Officials in your body can only function perfectly if they are at the right temperature. And the Three Heater governs the temperature that each of these Organs function at. Let us see what we can learn from this.

Suppose that they call it the Three Heater because the body is divided in three Jiao. Three Jiao means three divisions. You have the upper Jiao, the upper heater; the middle Jiao, and the lower Jiao.

Think of the not hundreds, but thousands, of diseases that are brought about as a result of a malfunction of the Three Heater. And there is a function that is not taught in orthodox medicine.

In the upper Jiao you have the Heart and you have the Lungs, and you have Circulation-Sex. Two Fire Organs and a Metal Organ. Suppose that this upper Jiao suddenly becomes very cold. Then these three Organs contract so you can't breathe. And you say, 'Well, it's asthma' (or some such silly name). Nothing of the sort! And people say, 'Oh, my heart,' because they are crushing it in to try to keep the warmth. And other people suddenly find, 'Gosh, my feet are going cold,' or, 'I can't get an erection.'

Now also, the mental symptoms begin to become imbalanced. You start to exhibit lack of joy, lack of Fire, lack of love. You exhibit the grief associated with Metal, plus you have got the physical part where you can hardly breathe when you have got terrible pains in your chest. But all you have got to do is to bring the heat back into that upper area, and both those Organs and the one Function will become perfectly normal. We just alter the thermostat.

Think of all the kidney, bladder, urinary, menstrual disorders, amenorrhoea, dysmenorrhoea, irregular menstruation, painful menstruations, excessive urination, inability to urinate, cramps in the lower part of the abdomen. If the lower Jiao goes cold and freezes, all these symptoms will be exhibited. You can have total sexual cut-off; constipation. The whole part is so frozen you have pain in passing water; you can't even pass water. The periods go totally irregular; there's no way that a woman can conceive. How many women pray for a child, and the only reason they can't conceive is because the lower Jiao is cold. No sperm is going to travel up there; that's no place for a child to be created —in an ice box. So out it goes. It has to be warm and comfortable.

But you see doctors treating kidney disorders, bladder disorders, anus disorders—all manner of things of that kind. Yet there is nothing wrong with these organs at all; increase the heat down there and every one of those symptoms disappears for good.

This frightens me! How many people are being treated for organic malfunctions when there is nothing wrong with the organs at all. It is simply because there is a malfunction of the Three Heater, whose job is to keep every organ in perfect harmony and balance temperature-wise.

Because we don't know anything about a Three Heater, how very foolish we are at times. We just take it for granted that the body is at a constant temperature all the time. What a marvellous job this function is doing. Even if we go out in the cold, in a few moments, instead of our body reproducing the cold that is outside, it stays the same. The skin surface might get a little cold, but, inside, we stay much the same temperature.

You go into a sauna where the heat is, oh my God, unforgiveable! Yet you don't fry inside; your body inside stays the same. And all this adjustment is the work of the Three Heater official, keeping your body and your mind and your spirit at that even temperature so that it can function normally. The lesson that we learn from this is to respect this Official and not abuse it. The idea of going into a sauna and then dumping yourself into an ice-cold swimming pool is just abusing this Official, saying, 'Now I'll steam you up. Now you work like hell to keep me cold.' So it does that, and you say, 'Right, now I'll have you the other way; I'm going into ice water, now you make me hot.' Crazy! Don't take hot baths, don't take cold baths. If you can try to take a bath at exactly body temperature, you are giving this Official all the respect that he is entitled to, and making his job a million times easier. It's a hard enough job to keep all parts of the body at an equal temperature. Very, very difficult indeed.

Now, self diagnosis. I don't believe in it; but one way in which you can physically ascertain the state of your Three Heater is by just touching. If you just put your hand on the upper Jiao—and you have to take your clothes off—don't do it now, otherwise they will say we are having an orgy; and I have only got one good suit—lay your hand on your upper Jiao, just gently. Then put it on your middle Jiao—just put your bottom, little finger about level with your umbilicus; that's your middle Jiao. Then put your hand on your lower Jiao. If your Three Heater is working well, then the temperatures should be identical. If you find one area is much colder or much hotter than another, then you know that your Three Heater is not functioning correctly.

But don't worry about it. This is an egg-hen situation, which always arises with traditional Chinese medicine. If you have a major malfunction of the Heart and the Lung—say they are hyperfunctioning—they in turn would pull down the temperature of the Three Heater. So, although your Three Heater may be imbalanced, that may not be the cause; it could be secondary. The symptoms would be the same.

On the other hand, if the Three Heater failed, then you would get cold in the upper Jiao. The same symptoms of the Three Heater would be the cause; and the Heart and Lungs would be secondary.

So you can't just feel and say, 'Oh, my Heart!' It may be your Three Heater. You can't feel and say, 'Oh, my Three Heater!' It may be your Lungs. You can't feel and say, 'Good heavens, this is wrong; it must be my Lungs or my Heart.' It could be Circulation-Sex. But it is valuable for you to be able to check the comparative temperatures of the three Jiao.

I always feel that one should have a do-it-yourself kit to go home with at the end of every seminar—although we haven't finished yet. I'm not finishing until you start going to the door. My plane doesn't go until seven o'clock in the morning, and I'm having a great time!

Look again at the circle of the Chinese Clock and look at the circle of the Five Elements. The energy is moving around all the time. So many people say, 'I am trying to get centred; I am trying to get myself round in a circle.' The centre is like the hub of a wheel. Everything is equidistant from the centre. Unless you have got perfect balance and harmony, you will go through life without perfect harmony of body, mind and spirit.

If the hub is off-centre—and you have seen clowns riding bikes with the hubs off-centre in the circus, and the wheel goes up and down—that's how your energy is going to go all the time. Up and down. The centre of your energy is found on the umbilicus, so when you get home tonight—I suggest you wait until you get home tonight—No, why not?—You may have some fun doing it here when we are over! Just go up to someone and say, 'Hey, can I test the centre of your energy?' All you need to do is to put your three main fingers and your thumb together, leaving a little hole in the middle. Put it centrally over the umbilicus. Press in; and you will feel a pulsation. That pulsation should come so that you just feel it equally on each of the three fingers and thumb.

What is likely to happen is that you will feel it excessively to the north, to the east, to the south or to the west. There is no point in you trying to create balance and harmony in the whole system unless the centre is in the centre. What you can do is centre your own centre, by very gently massaging it back towards the centre of the umbilicus. That in itself is a classic treatment. You then will centre your own energy. Nature can help to balance; but Nature can never balance if your centre of energy is off. How can Nature balance when you have got the hub out of the centre?

You see, one of the things I like about traditional Chinese medicine—and probably this is what brought me into it for the second time, or my second life—is that it is a great fun thing. It's a system of medicine that gives you an immediate contact with a human being, with perfectly legitimate reasons.

We discussed earlier the Chinese pulses which represent the ten Organs and two Functions in your body. Six of the Organs are represented on your left hand—the Heart, Small Intestines, the Liver and Gall Bladder, the Bladder and the Kidney. On the right, you have the Lungs and the Colon, Stomach and Spleen, Three Heater and Circulation-Sex. By palpating those twelve pulses, we can tell exactly how every Function in your body is working.

As I have said, learning to read pulses takes a whole lifetime. You may have heard of many ancient Chinese who were able to read pulses according to the classic teachings. Just by reading the pulses, they can not only tell you more about yourself than you can tell them, they can tell from the Chinese pulses what has been, what is, and what is going to be. This is not fortune telling, not gazing into the future; it is reading exactly the state of each of the Organs and Functions.

It's very difficult to be able to read the twelve pulses. It takes several years to read the twelve pulses. It takes several years to read them meaningfully. When I then tell you that every pulse has twenty-eight different qualities, you are taking on a task of reading twelve pulses twenty-eight times each. That's why it takes a lifetime!

If you can discern those twenty-eight qualities, then you need nothing else at all. You needn't bother over the colour, the sound, the odour, the emotion; you don't even need a case history. You can establish immediately the Causative Factor.

I have been studying this system of medicine—and I still am very much a student—for over thirty years, and I am just about up to twenty-six qualities. I reckon perhaps in ten more years I may make the twenty-eight; that goes to show you the complexity. But isn't it fascinating to know what your own body is prepared to tell you if you put in the effort to try to listen, to look, to feel and to hear? The body is telling us its needs. We are not thinking about what we want, but finding out what the body needs.

Another thing I like about this system is this. This young lady down here . . . I have had my eye on her ever since she came! Under normal circumstances, I suppose, when the day was over, I would have to go up and say, 'Do you come here often?' And she would say, 'Oh, no; and I'm not coming again!' All that sort of thing! But what I can do now is go down and say, 'Excuse me, darling; can I just take your pulses?' You see, that's giving me physical contact within ten seconds. If you know a system of medicine that will give you an introduction better than that . . . ! I've got her hand, and it's all legal. That's lovely!

And, of course, I can turn to her and say, 'Oh, my golly; your Gall Bladder doesn't feel too good!' No, it's perfect, really! I never tell anybody what is wrong with them. You are wonderful, perfect!

But, about one o'clock in the morning, if you see me leaving her apartment I don't want you thinking anything! I mean, I was just adjusting her Gall Bladder at the maximum period of activity. That in itself is reason for people to want to study this system of medicine. Everything becomes legal!

But I'll be *very truthful* with you. When I am talking about this system of medicine, I am truthful; I only lie when I am joking!

We talk about vital Qi energy, and feeling the energy and the connection between the cosmic energy and us, and the energy that is transmitted from one person to another. You can be in a room talking to your friends and someone comes in through that door, someone perhaps you don't particularly like. You say, 'God, I wish he hadn't come.' The whole atmosphere changes; just through the presence of that person.

Or, you can be in a situation where the whole

presence of the room becomes alive by someone coming in. 'Wow! He's here!' And that shows how your own physical energy manifests and affects every person you come into contact with. It's tremendous.

Look at a little baby: how aware he is of this energy. A baby can be over here and the mother can come in through the door silently. The baby does not need to turn his head. He knows his mother is there. He picks up the vibrations immediately.

Wait until one of your friends has just had a little baby. Suppose you are not really fond of babies, and you go and pick it up and say, 'Ah, isn't he beautiful?' The baby will scream its head off, as if to say, 'Don't play your silly games with me!' Watch this. If you really do love that baby, and even if it's really crying, and you really love it, and you pick it up, that baby will know in a minute and stop crying. That is how sensitive we all were when we were born.

Why do we throw these gifts away? Especially when the body is trying to tell us so much. Realise what I was saying earlier on about vision. Many of us may say, 'Well, I don't like the world as it is. I don't like this, and I don't like that.' I would suggest that is judging the world through limited vision. If you will allow natural expansion, you will be overwhelmed with life; it's just so fascinating. And if you're not going through life sharing any of that, I don't know why you are going on. It's a complete waste of time.

Time for tea. I haven't got a Chinese Clock, but this fellow's sudden gasping and changing of colour down here shows that, if he doesn't get one of those cigarettes soon, he's not going to last out! And my love for him is such that he can go and have a cigarette; and that gives all the others of you an excuse; me too.

After Tea

What I feel I would like to do now is briefly cover one or two things that are very, very important—things that perhaps we have previously taken for granted—so that we can see again how, through not understanding how our own body, mind and spirit function, we really don't understand many of the things that Nature and God have given us. We cause a vast amount of disease *ourselves*.

We can see how, often, our body is describing an organic malfunction to us in a variety of different ways. On the Five Element chart, you saw the five major colours—red, yellow, white, blue and green. If you get a major organic imbalance, then not only will you love and crave for a season, or hate a season, but you will detest that colour; no way, for example, can you wear it.

Many of you who are a little bit over twenty-one can look back and see times in your life when you loved being in red; now you can't stand it. You loved being in green, and now you can't stand it; once you hated blue, now you love it. Yet, if you are reasonably balanced in body, mind and spirit, each colour has gifts to give you. It has its own effect on your mind and your body, and you can appreciate all of the colours at different times as you can appreciate all of the seasons. Your like or dislike for a specific colour, and craving or hating a specific colour, is very often a manifestation in your own body, mind or spirit of an Element which is imbalanced.

We take colour for granted. What we don't realise is that there are radiations and emanations that come from colour which affect your vital Qi energy.

If you want to prove this one, then I suggest that you go into a room, set the thermostat shall we say at 68°, you would start to shiver and goose pimples would come on your skin. But at exactly the same 68°, if you go into a room with red walls and stand on a red carpet, you will perspire. That gives you your own factual proof of the effect of colour upon your own well-being.

Do you see how crazy we are because we don't recognise this and don't respect it? What we do, if we have, for the sake of simplicity, a major malfunction in the Metal Element—which would be the Lungs or the Colon—we then need to have yellow to support it. Mother/child; the child is sick, so you increase the energy of the Mother.

I wonder how many people, when they go to bed, sleep between white sheets? I venture to suggest that 85% to 90% of the population do. You may thus be in touch with vital radiation and emanation coming from the colour which is making your imbalance worse when you are in bed. Colour does influence your life. It does influence your vital Qi energy.

Consider the garments you wear closest to yourself, those that are in contact with your energy directly. Most people have white under-vests and white pants. This can be absolutely crazy!

If you were to find that you are very, very cold at night in bed, but then you slept between red sheets, I venture you would perspire and be very hot. *Vice versa*. If you were very, very hot between blue sheets, the influence of that colour is so dynamic, it affects every minute of your night . . . and following day.

I wonder how many of us are exposing ourselves to colours which are making it very difficult for our bodies to overcome disease naturally? If you change the colour, it assists the body to overcome the disease. The thing that you have to remember—and this is very humbling, but it's very gratifying to be able to say it—there is not a man or a woman on the face of this earth who can cure anything. That is a very sweeping statement, but factual. I repeat, there is not a man or a woman on the face of this earth who can cure a cough, an itch, or anything. The only thing we can do is assist Nature in what only Nature can do. We use our skills and experiences to assist Nature; man doesn't cure the disease. Nature cures the disease.

In my country years ago, there was, and still is a specific therapy that is simple colour therapy. Anyone who has studied colour therapy intensely—it's not very simple—can see that certain radiations of colour enable the patient to overcome diseases. That's the power of the patient to overcome diseases. That's the power of colour. We can do a lot now to recognise what colours feel comfortable to us.

If you still don't believe colour affects you, I'll give you a better example. I can quote this in America but not in England. When you go to a dinner dance and a knees-up in England, and you are going to have a rocking evening, everyone goes in a black evening suit, you know, with a white shirt and a black tie. But, here, you see they go in yellow, they go in red, all gorgeous colours. The men are like peacocks; they look beautiful! At home, it's all black! You can be different, as long as you wear black!

So, you go out for a good night's dancing; you girls put on a red dress, and you men put on your red jackets. You get on the dance floor at eight o'clock. I gamble, by half-past-eleven, you will be saying, 'Come on, I think we'd better go now; goodness I'm buggered!' (or you may use a more polite word . . . Like saying, 'I'm shattered,' or what ever it might be). But, if you put on a black gown, and you put on black evening dress, you will go on dancing until three o'clock in the morning. The colour has made that difference to your vital energy. Try it, and when you know it works, then you will pay more respect to the colours you wear. And, if you find that you feel more comfortable in a specific colour, then, O.K., stay with it for a while.

But, again; it's not quite that simple; because when you first start to become imbalanced you crave a certain colour. That is nature instinctively telling you, 'Hey, wear green.' And you say, 'God, I didn't like green. Now I do.' What you are trying to do by using that colour green is support the malfunction of your Liver and Gall Bladder. If you are getting hyperfunctioning of the Heart, there is no way you can wear red; and you mustn't wear red, because it will increase the hyperfunctioning. Therefore you will wear yellow or blue, because blue controls fire.

Then, you spend most of your time in bed. You shouldn't do, because excess of it is a total waste of time. There's much fun to be had up and about—although you can have some fun in bed, so I have heard; but that's beside the point! You spend much time between the sheets and it is important for you to experiment, and try sleeping between different coloured sheets. I gamble you will notice a difference. Try it; honestly, it's a good investment. You needn't all buy five pairs of sheets. If there are ten of your friends, buy five sets between you and all of you try them out. Not at the same time . . . separately! You will feel a tremendous difference. You will wake up one morning and say, 'Hey, my God, I haven't woken up like this before for ages. I feel rested. I feel much more energetic.' That's the effect of colour.

Another thing, since you are spending a lot of time in your home . . . it is very important that you decorate the inside of your home so that the radiations and emanations from colour make that home a welcoming, life-giving place. People go into their homes and suddenly collapse. Collapse in your own home? If you have the wrong colours in your home you will hit the deck. If you have the right colours in the home then, in no time, suddenly your energy will resurge. That's the effect of colour. It is dynamic.

Of course, you may not know what colours are advantageous to you and what colours are not advantageous to you, because, initially, as imbalance gets worse—we were mentioning green helping the Liver and Gall Bladder—then the colour could be worsening the disease. So, at one stage it can help you; and, at another stage, it can help to destroy you, or help you to become more sick. So you need to experiment with colours to see which you feel more at home with. Whereas white may be beneficial for me, it may destroy Oscar here; red may be very beneficial for Oscar and may destroy me. We are unique individuals. We need to know what colours are supporting us, making us feel good.

The only colour that has positive radiations for every person is aubergine. You may say, 'Aubergine; what the hell's that?' Yes, what is it? It's virtually eggplant colour, purplish. So, if you are doubtful as to what colour you need, then have some aubergine in the room where you are sleeping. Just aubergine curtains! You needn't do the whole room in aubergine. Then you will have permanent, positive radiations which can influence your total well-being.

Colour is really devastating. So change your underpants, change your vest. Go for reds and the blues and the greens, and the yellows and the whites. See if you feel different. Change your shirts, change your dresses. Don't stay all the time in these blue jeans and blue what have you. Oh no! I know they may be very convenient; but, if needs be, dye the jeans red, or yellow, or some other colour; but don't just stay in blue jeans. You are exposing yourself far too much to the radiation from that colour and it will sap your energy. The longer you wear it, the more it will sap your energy and the more lethargic you will become. You will be less vibrant because you cannot be exposed to blue constantly. So flip the colours around, particularly where they come into contact with the skin. I know you don't wear pyjamas—and I understand some Americans don't wear underpants either—so, if you have got blue jeans, look what you are touching with all this ice-cold, negative energy! It is well worth thinking about! Women with vaginal discharges, with vaginal irritation, even with irregular menstruations, must wear cotton. You must never wear nylon or man-made fibres; not in contact with your body, and you may find, just by changing to natural fibre underpants that many of these disturbing things you suffer from will, by themselves, start to get right. That's the power of colour and natural materials.

These simple things are very extensive in effect. I just want you to realise the available energy from different sources, that we need to recognise and understand. Now you understand why you really loved that red dress ten years ago, yet no way could you wear it now. That is telling you something.

We had a particular casebook back home, not so many weeks ago. I had the privilege of taking a group of my students through their clinical training. They had just finished two years of their practical training. We had a particular woman who had a major Fire imbalance, and she had got white underpants, white bra, a white slip, white skirt and a white top. She had also mentioned that she hated red. And there she was, putting herself in all this white, which basically was making her condition so much worse. And they treated this woman. I mean, they are great masters, the students; when they are in those first three weeks of clinic, they do things I wish to God that I could do after thirty years!

They treated this woman twice, and she didn't even go home the second time. She went straight into a department store. Now, we hadn't spoken to her about colour at all. You mustn't put ideas into patient's heads, otherwise they don't do things naturally. She went and bought red pants, a red bra, a red slip and a red dress—after we had started to increase her Fire. She came back the next week and said, 'You know, I went mad when I left here last week. I have never done anything so stupid in my life. I went and bought all these red things, and I have never worn red.' 'But,' she said, 'they are great, wonderful. I wish I had done it before.' Ninety percent of the trouble had gone. Isn't that amazing? That again shows how subconsciously you go on and off colours because of their power. That's something you can help yourself with.

The last thing I would like you to give some credence to—something that crops up in everybody's mind sooner or later—is diet.

We live from the food that we get from our Mother and the air that we breathe from our Father; and that is how we survive. And once we have corrected the imbalances of disease, the only way to keep healthy is to pay due recognition to your Mother and Father. For the food that you eat governs your energy factor, as does the air you breathe.

As I have already told you, I don't believe in diets, not 'people's diets', but I do believe in diet. Individually tailored diets to the needs of one specific person. There is no such thing as a people's diet. It is not that easy. That's why somebody goes on a diet and says, 'Hey, it made me feel great,' yet somebody else goes on it, and you say, 'How did it make you feel?' 'Oh, my God, dreadful!' It's the wrong fuel in the wrong body. What is good for one body and one mind is not good for all others.

Diet is very, very important. This is where naturopathic doctors play a very important part. They study the needs of each individual; then give the fuel for that body. You don't put paraffin in your motor car, you put gasoline— the right fuel for the particular vehicle.

So one is in a dilemma. 'What do I eat?' Some people say, 'Eat a load of rice.' Some people say, 'Well, don't eat at all.' Some people say, 'Well, eat a load of fruit.' It's all very confusing.

If you believe, as I believe, that God in his wisdom knows far more, then you will see that in his wisdom he provided the food for the environment in which we live. All energy and environment are one; and we are one with that environment and that energy. So eat the food in the area in which you live, in the season in which it grows, and that way you are one hundred percent safe.

Of course, if you have a serious disease, that in itself may not be enough or appropriate. You may need to add to the base or take away from it. But as a general parameter, trust in Nature. That is why, in England, we don't grow any oranges. This is why we grow more starchy foods, and why in hot climates they grow less starchy foods. You have already seen how we have the Element Wood within us; and you see that the Wood in our particular environment is also part of us, a manifestation, a medium of energy. The macrocosm again and the microcosm. So, keep in tune with Nature by eating the food in the season in which it grows. That is the best yardstick for health. There may be occasions when we should borrow someone else's food, for a certain disease, in order that we can help the patient to recover; but that is very much the exception.

If you want the broad spectrum of this, take the Masai warriors, who are an extremely strong, very powerful, very virile race. Their basic diet many years ago was red ox blood. Then there are the Eskimos. They too are very tenacious and very strong, tremendous people. They live virtually on blubber. Change the two diets and you would wipe out both races. These are the extremes. We come somewhere between.

Fly to a foreign country. You immediately start to eat their food. Your body doesn't know what the hell to do with it. It's not your environment. So you may become sick. Do remember that.

The other important aspect about food is that, as you study traditional Chinese medicine, you find that it is not what you eat that really matters, but what is happening to what you eat.

The Small Intestine, in traditional Chinese medicine, is the Official which separates the pure from the impure. Every mortal thing that goes through our mouths contains some purity, and some impurity. It is this Official's job to separate out what the body needs, and to discard what the body does not need by sending it on to the Colon to evacuate.

Therefore it doesn't really matter *what* you eat. You must know people who live on junk food—they have hamburgers and Coke and MacDonald's chips and all that sort of thing—and they are as healthy as can be. And you will know others, on a very staid strict diet, buying health foods and mint tea and all that other garbage, and they can hardly make it to the health food shop, they are so ruddy exhausted. The former have perfect Separators of Pure from Impure, so that no matter what is eaten, they can extract that essence of quality which will drive the body. The others are eating whole food, but, if their Small Intestine Officials are sick, they cannot separate the pure from the impure, so they are getting the garbage as well as the pure food.

So, more important than diet is what is happening to the food when it goes inside. Your Small Intestine is really the prerequisite for a healthy body-mind; the food comes second. We usually thought food came first. It doesn't. It's what happens to the food that comes first.

Some little kids used to walk about in my early days, with no shoes on, with no socks on, holes in their trousers, going round the coal yard, sometimes sucking coal—and never had a sniffle. They never had a cold. And yet other kids, whose mothers protected them, and wrapped them up, and gave them all the best of everything, they caught every mortal thing that was going. Those little rugged kids had obviously got damn good Separators—you know, they could even get something from coal. At least they got minerals, and we need minerals and trace elements. They could use some essence out of it which would be dangerous for someone else to eat. That shows the whole essence of the respectability of food. *It's what happens to the food you eat that matters.*

But obviously, even if you have got a well-balanced Small Intestine, eating good food puts less strain on this Official, and thus you become even more healthy. But keep it in mind—don't tell your best friend to go on your diet.

And, now, the very last thing of all . . . looks like I wrote two things here. Ah! One I wrote to remind myself. When I went into my hotel, the receptionist said, 'Will you write your name?' And I said, 'I'm sorry, I can't write.' He said, 'It doesn't matter, I can't read!'

No here we are . . . herbs. Herbs play a tremendously important role in America. This is something that needs a lot of thought. Tremendous adverts for ginseng. 'Do you want virility?' 'Do you want strength?' and all this sort of thing. 'Have ginseng!' You must be joking!

Ginseng is a very valuable herb. Tremendously valuable in the country in which it grows. A lot of people say,

'Well, I want to study Chinese herbology.' Why? You are not Chinese. You are not living in a Chinese culture. The herbs are growing in the Chinese environment, and the Lord in his wisdom grew them there for the Chinese people, and the Japanese, and the Koreans. Over here, you see, we have another system of herbology: American Indian herbology is based on the herbs right for you people. The environment in which you grow is the environment in which the right herbs for you grow. In South America, the same thing happens. The Chinese have reached a sort of zenith of herbology. The reason it rings in peoples' minds is because to become a traditional Chinese herbologist you have to study exactly the same as a traditional acupuncturist does. Whereas we use needles to balance the energy, they use herbs. But they do all the diagnosis exactly the same; and, furthermore, when they give the herbs, they generally give them within an hour of their being picked.

I can remember many years ago, when I was with a very famous Chinese herbologist, a traditional one, he used to send his apprentices out to various mountain sources and various fields, and they had to wait almost hour by hour until the particular herb had reached a correct Yin/Yang balance. One hour too late and the herb was useless; one hour too early and the herb was useless. It really is very technical. It's very skilled. Even after being picked, the herb would have to be compounded and given to the patient within an hour or so. It is a brilliant, brilliant system.

The tragedy with English herbology, and American Indian herbology, is that the practitioners haven't got the intricate skill of doing traditional diagnosis so that they can give a herb for a specific element or a specific meridian. What they tend to do is use herbology as a blanket cover.

So those of you who are trying to revitalise yourself on some other nationality's herbs, I suggest you think again. Remember, nature knows better than we do. Heed the call of Nature. If you want to use herbs, which are fantastic, go to a good herbologist and make sure you are taking the herbs that are grown in your own country. You have some dynamic herbs and great herbologists here in America.

So there we are. I am a little bit biased in thinking that acupuncture, traditional acupuncture, is the most beautiful system of medicine in the world. But I do not want to leave you in any doubt; I also feel that orthodox Western medicine, chiropractic, naturopathy, homoeopathy, osteopathy are equally good. But, again, any system of medicine is only as good as the person who is practising it. We have many Western doctors practising medicine who should be in jail. We have many chiropractors practising medicine who should be in jail . . . and acupuncturists, and others.

So, ignoring the worst and taking the best, there really is no difference between the motivation of a genuine Western medical practitioner, a genuine naturopath, and a genuine acupuncturist: they take up that job because they love to help people who are sick, and each system of medicine has its valid points.

There is no panacea. Traditional acupuncture is not a panacea; orthodox medicine is not a panacea. If they were, there would be nobody sick in the world. Every system of medicine has something to offer. So don't decry one system to praise another. You may decry an individual who is practising it badly, but a good Western doctor is as valuable as a good traditional acupuncturist. A good osteopath, a good naturopath, a good herbalist—they are all of equal worth. Keep a sense of proportion. I hear people say, 'I wouldn't go to a bloody Western doctor.' Not much they wouldn't . . . until they go head on in a car accident and have broken their legs; or they are suffering from internal haemorrhaging. Then they thank God the Western doctor comes along and saves their lives. So keep that sense of proportion. And do remember, again, it is not the doctor's responsibility! It is *your* responsibility, to help to maintain your own healthy body, mind and spirit, just as you maintain your little motor car.

Now, I know there are some of you who wish to ask questions. As you know unfortunately I have a patient waiting for me. I am sorry about this but it is an emergency. I must sincerely say that this is one of the nicest groups I have ever spoken to in the whole of my life. I appreciate what you have given me. I would like to stay with you but, much as I love you, a patient in distress must come before you, and I will have to get to the hotel to see her in about another three-quarters-of-an-hour. So, if any of you have any specific questions you would like to ask me, I will do my best to try to answer them briefly.

I do find questions can be a sort of dampening down, an anti-climax. Really, I like to finish with jokes and make everybody laugh and go out saying, 'Isn't it good?' I don't want you to say, 'Oh my God, what did that person want to ask that for?' Because then you will go out with negative feelings and we will forget all the joy and love we have shared during the course of the day. So, if you can, don't get the questions too personal. You know, 'I have got haemorrhoids, what can I do?' My answer is, 'Go to your physician; or go to your traditional acupuncturist, and ask him.' So, general questions please which will be of benefit for everyone.

Questions

Yes, my friend?

To what degree would you say that acupuncture is taking hold in this country?

I say it is making very rapid strides. The first thing that brought me to America was an endeavour to do a one man crusade, going to Senate meetings, and running around America saying, 'For God's sake, ban it! Don't allow anyone to practise it!' Because the people here were doing local doctor, and I could envisage they were causing more disease than they were helping.

There is no need for first-aid acupuncture in a place like America. Why should a first class physician become a tenth rate first-aid man? If you are going to have acupuncture in this country, then, for heaven's sake, let's make sure it is of a quality which the people are entitled to.

I was offered hundreds and hundreds of thousands of dollars to certify people to practise after a hundred hour training course. Well, that's crazy! It is taking my people ten years to get a doctorate. Are you going to sacrifice that for a thousand dollars? Of course you can't learn it in one hundred hours. You can't learn it totally in a lifetime. You certainly can learn enough to help people at the end of three or four years, and then more so at the end of five, and more so at the end of six.

People in this country, sick people, should not be exploited; but they are being exploited by local doctor acupuncture. Thank heavens, many States are now setting up registration boards. I don't think the quality and the standards they are asking for are high enough, but at least they have set an established level. Why shouldn't they? I mean, you are playing with somebody else's body, mind and spirit. And because you are a well-trained Western physician, it doesn't mean to say that you are a miracle man—that you can learn acupuncture in one hundred hours when it is taking somebody else ten years. I wouldn't turn round and suggest that I could do Western medicine in one hundred hours; I would have to study solidly for six years.

Fortunately, now, we have enough graduates here, trained at the College of Traditional Acupuncture in England, for traditional acupuncture in this country to become properly established.

Five years ago, probably twenty or thirty thousand people were practising local doctor. O.K., you can sell something for a while on a gimmick; but gimmicks don't last. Now, all the flash courses are diminishing. Whereas, two or three years ago, you could pick up any magazine and see fifty local doctor seminars going on—for a hundred hours training—now, you don't see *one*. People understand and discriminate. People are now looking for traditional acupuncturists. And there are enough in this country now to make sure that it's firmly established forever. They are going to give the quality of medicine that people are entitled to. All the others have been exploitation of sick people. That is the biggest crime in the world—when someone is sick, to exploit them. It's worse than murder.

Yes, my friend?

One of the concerns I have heard raised about acupuncture is that a continued use of a point with the needle will build up scar tissue. Is that so?

No. That is a misconception. First of all, if you remember early on, I said that a practitioner would never treat two patients the same because each is uniquely individual. Also, a traditional practitioner hardly ever uses the same point twice. Local doctors use the same point all the time. Their 'cook book' says, 'Use Lung 7, Lung 7, Lung 7, Lung 7.' Eventually they will destroy that point. They will affect that point, or imbalance that point, so that it can never recover. A traditional acupuncturist never does that.

You see, once you have used a point, that takes a person from this position to that position. If you use that point again, you are taking the person back to this position. There are 360 points in the body. Each has a different meaning, a different spirit and a different connotation. Each one will take a person by selective choice to the next—from A to B, A to B, A to B. What are you waiting for? There's no point in that; so we move on.

Again, look at the acupuncture points as we use them in the West. We say, 'Circulation-Sex 8,' which we call a Fire point. We are using Roman numerals, and saying Fire point. But the Chinese had a character; and that character told a story; and it told a story about that point. This again is awesome—how much they knew the needs of people. A picture can tell you far better than words. Words are garbage; pictures tell you; feelings tell you.

That point we call 'Circulation-Sex 8, Fire point,' they call the Palace of Weariness. Each point has a spirit. So what do they mean by the Palace of Weariness? Five thousand years ago, the Chinese saw a palace as being the house of God. Their emperor, who in those days was God, had the power of life and death. The joy or the distress of the nation was dependent upon the emperor, or their God. Many people put their God in that palace. They saw that palace as being totally worthy of this ultimate great person. Everything is in there—an abundance of love, of caring, an abundance of food, of wine. So many patients, who are really, really sick, just get so weary with their disease that they just can't fight it any more. The Chinese say bring them into the Palace of Weariness. They are tired, and it will feed them, and it will bathe them. It's not going to cure them, but they are going to come out revitalised.

A traditional acupuncturist has to study the spirit of every point. Is this patient waiting for the Palace of Weariness? Is this the time to use it; or do I use it the next time? Or does he want the Lesser Palace first? Or does he want the Spirit Gate opening first? Or does he need the Gate of Hope opening first? Or does he need to go into the Blazing Valley first?

Local doctors say, 'Circulation-Sex 8, Circulation-Sex 8, Circulation-Sex 8.' They don't understand that there is a spirit there. The wisdom and the depth in this system of medicine is such that, after you have taken them into the Palace of Weariness, would you need to take them in again? No, you wouldn't. Perhaps you would need to bathe them in the Heavenly Pond. You may need to open the Windows of the Sky—so that they can see that there is a future, that there is life. The spirits of the points are like a fairy story—but it works. And the patients can tell you which points they need. 'God, I wish I could see. I really wish I could see.' So, open up the Windows of the Sky, so that they can see. 'There's no hope doctor; I just, I just give up.' So, open up the Gate of Hope, to give them hope. Once again, as I have said repeatedly, actually it's not that simple. Symptoms can hide the Causative Factor. We may find that it's the child screaming for the Gate of Hope and what is really needed is opening of the Inner Frontier Gate belonging to the mother —which then, in turn, will open the Gate of Hope. So it does become very complicated—not as simple as it first sounds —but you will never use an acupuncture point repeatedly. Only local doctors do that, and they should be banned, horsewhipped, shot—but with loving bullets!

Praise for Professor J.R. Worsley and *J.R. Worsley Talking About Acupuncture in New York*

"J.R. Worsley was a true Master of Classical Five-Element Acupuncture, the most alive, dynamic and inspirational teacher I have ever come across and the best Father a daughter could ever wish for. I feel *so* grateful to have had him in my life as both a teacher and Father. What a gift."

—**Hilary Skellon**, Director,
Institute of Taoist Education and Acupuncture

"A magician once said that acupuncture and magic have much in common. How true, for how can it be that a needle, as slender as a hair, inserted into the body, can clear a befuddled mind and put a sparkle in your eye. The practice of J.R. Worsley's Classical Five-Element Acupuncture can do just that. In this wonderful book, J.R. Worsley outlines the basic Laws of the ancient tradition in a fascinating, lively conversation of modern everyday life. J.R.'s unique spirit, his love, his understanding of Nature, his passion, humor and knowledge, leap off the page into our hearts, inspiring us with the richness of this natural and profound system of medicine. This book is a must for everyone."

—**Erica J. Apollo**, Co-organizer of J.R. Worsley's
Seminar: *J.R. Talking About Acupuncture in New York*

"I typed the original version of *J.R. Worsley Talking About Acupuncture in New York*. When I read it now, I still laugh and learn so much. He has given a priceless gift to all. "

—**Maureen Postins**, England

"Professor J.R. Worsley was recognized by his teachers, colleagues, students and patients as a true Master of Classical Five-Element Acupuncture because of his brilliant understanding and mastery of this system of medicine. Hearing a tape of these lectures opened my heart to a completely new understanding of those I love and myself. I was so taken with his warmth, compassion and total dedication to helping patients that I resolved to study with him and practice this medicine myself. Now, twenty years later, I am one of hundreds of his students who aspire to treat our patients with the clarity, depth and humility of our beloved teacher and mentor, J.R. This fascinating book is filled with his wisdom, humor and joy of life."

—**David Goodell**, President, Worsley Institute of Classical Five-Element Acupuncture

"For twenty-four years, J.R. Worsley was my teacher and my inspiration to become the best I could be: an instrument of healing. This wonderful book captures the spontaneous joy of J.R.'s wit, wisdom and timeless truth."

—**Neil R. Gumenick**, Founder and Director, Institute of Classical Five-Element Acupuncture Inc.

"Titles such as Professor, Master, Doctor, and Renowned Teacher do not begin to encompass the brilliance and enormity of Professor J.R. Worsley's work. He made an unparalleled contribution to the field of medicine: resurrecting and presenting to the world the spirit and practice of an ancient system of medicine that was nearly lost. He was a great teacher, a true master, warm, full of humor and yet uncompromising in the absolute integrity of his teaching. I will forever feel grateful to have had the good fortune to study with him."

—Khosrow Khalighi,
Founder and Director of the
Five Elements Training School

"Camarado, this is no book, who touches this touches a person.
I spring from the pages into your arms . . ."
—Walt Whitman

"I was there when our beloved teacher, Dr. Worsley, spoke these words in this book. With and without acupuncture needles, in his presence the simple, joyful beauty of being alive shined. Read and know your own joy in this, his written presence."

—Dianne Connelly, Co-Founder of Tai Sophia
Institute for the Healing Arts

"I am honored and privileged to have studied with Dr. Worsley in the later years of his life, when his humanity, his love for the work of the Five Elements, patients, family and Judy simply shined. Words he spoke in one of his last lectures in May 2003 are priceless to me. Thank you, J.R."

—Diane McCormick, M.D.

"Professor J.R. Worsley was an extraordinary teacher, clinician and healer in the highest sense of the words. His ability to inspire his students and love his patients is legendary. The world will not see the likes of someone like him for a long time. It will always be my honor and privilege to have known him."

—Robert J. Abramson, D.D.S., M.D.
Co-Director, The Five-Element Group of New York

"I had no idea that first weekend seminar in January 1974 in LA with J.R. Worsley would so completely change the course of my life forever. I am totally blessed to be a student of his for 29 years. He taught me all I know about acupuncture. I now have an incredible treasure inside me, which no one can take away. God bless you, J.R., I miss you dearly."

—Jeffrey D. Kauffman, M.D.

"Dr. J.R. Worsley has brought to the modern world the gift of Five Element Acupuncture, a system of healing that profoundly touches body, mind and spirit. His teachings and clinical acumen have created an organized method to allow anyone seriously interested in using this ancient healing system a means to be effective in treating patients. Dr. Worsley has inspired me to continue teaching this system to physicians as well as using it as a major part of my medical practice. This book brings to the general public his insight and understanding of the application of these poetic and powerful concepts of traditional Chinese thought to everyday life."

—Charles A. Moss, M.D.
Five Element Acupuncture Physician
Training Program

"J.R. Worsley was a dear friend as well as my acupuncturist for over 30 years. We met in England when he was in private practice. At that time, I worked each summer for Spectrum, a London growth center, as a consultant. Almost every client I met encouraged me to meet J.R. I was impressed by his popularity and the admiration he received. So we met.

"I am here attempting to convey to you what an extraordinary person, friend, teacher, and acupuncturist J.R. was. How youthful, honorable, humble, loving and decent he was. It was I who wrote the letter of introduction for Judy Becker to enter his acupuncture training course. I take pride in my success, for she was accepted, as well as take pleasure in the fact that she won his heart, for they eventually married. I am sad that J.R. is no longer with us. I miss him every day. I know how his great wit and insight would make me laugh and I take solace and comfort in how lucky I am to have known him so well."

—Marty Fromm, Professor of Psychology,
Miami Dade Jr. College; Gestalt Therapist

"This inspiring book captures the deep truth, universality and simplicity of this classical acupuncture system. Dr. J.R. Worsley brought these teachings to life for our time, and his words in this book have brought the man and his teachings to life for so many of my students and patients."

—Ronald Puhky, M.D.
Five Element Acupuncture Physician
Training Program

"On any other subject the man, J.R. Worsley, is a mere mortal, but ah, when he speaks on acupuncture—Classical Chinese Acupuncture—you are swept inexorably into another world, one of such eloquence, clarity and understanding that surely God must be speaking through him."

—Mark Penzer, J.R.'s friend and attorney

"What an amazing man, J.R. Worsley! He was funny, courageous, truthful, perceptive and kind. He knew we could be the best practitioners possible of this most beautiful system of healing called Classical Five-Element Acupuncture. Professor Worsley was determined to save this medicine from extinction, which thank goodness he did. His efforts to prepare future generations of practitioners, teachers and a designated Master, Judy Worsley, to carry the lineage forward, were supreme. It was my exceptional good fortune to have been his student and Apprentice."

—Suzanne Burnell

"J.R. had an innate understanding of the wisdom of Asian philosophy and its emphasis on the power of Nature to heal. He believed in this power and reminded us often that we only serve Nature. Nature does the healing. He sought, fiercely, to preserve this tradition that sees each person as more than an assembly of parts or symptoms. J.R. was a patient advocate in the deepest sense. He was not satisfied with helping only a part of a person. J.R. wanted everything for them: a complete, vital, full life. He wanted the best from them as well. They responded as we all do when our deepest selves are touched with genuine love and concern: they got better."

—**Joseph Soprani**

"This book shines with the wisdom, humor and brilliance of a true Master."

—**Beverly Heller**, Class of '73

"The world is truly a more beautiful, graceful, harmonious and healthy world because of what J.R. Worsley carried and shared with such devotion, faith and love. What a beautiful and courageous man. His work opened my heart. Thank you and God bless you, J.R."

—**Joyce Netishen**, Herbalist

"The gift that J.R. Worsley has given us is truly a gem. It addresses every human being's deepest pursuit for health and happiness."

—**Jan Blackmore**, Director, Institute of Classical Acupuncture, Inc.; President, Center for Acupuncture Research and Education, Inc.

"J.R. Worsley taught me there is always time to keep learning and to have compassion. He was a powerful teacher."

—Mary Ellen Metke

"I attended this lecture by Dr. Worsley in New York, and can testify that it made a huge impression on me. I still remember walking around the city during Saturday's lunch break after he told us we would feel better if we walked outside and breathed in the heavenly chi from the fresh air than if we ate lunch. This book is full of fresh information and is itself a "breath of fresh air". Well written and funny, it's for anyone interested in Acupuncture and in living a healthier life-style and feeling better."

—Frances Korbly-Canter

"Not just a 'good read' but also a life changing book which offers challenges to current concepts of health."

—Liz Pinder-Ayers

"Being a student and a patient of J.R. Worsley's impacted my life beyond measure. I have so much gratitude for his teaching and his steadfastness."

—Diane Macchiavelli

"From the moment I first met J.R., he has inspired me, both as a patient and practitioner of Classical Five-Element Acupuncture. His insights on the real possibility of life in harmony and balance have transformed my life and therefore, the lives of my patients. J.R. taught me as a practitioner to leave my ego outside the treatment room, to get out of the way, to be an instrument of Nature. And consequently, I have never had so much fun! Thank you J.R. With his wife, Judy Worsley, now as Master of this wonderful system of medicine, his legacy is in safe hands. J.R. successfully fulfilled his responsibilities as Master: to transmit the teachings to the next generation. I believe he will rest in peace knowing that."

—Declan Rothwell

"The kind of Acupuncture that Dr. Worsley taught and practiced is nothing short of miraculous. Until our daughter, Julia, was two years old, she was not able to sleep more than four hours per day. We had tried everything to help her. Then we took her for an acupuncture consultation and treatment from Dr. Worsley. That night, for the first time in her life, she slept eight hours. Her life changed and so did her parents! A year later, an acupuncturist asked her if she remembered her treatment. "Yes", she said, "Before I met Dr. Worsley, my spirit was in a box. Afterwards, my spirit filled the whole world!" What wonderful medicine! What a wonderful man! Thank you Dr. Worsley for your loyalty to this ancient healing tradition of Classical Five-Element Acupuncture."

—Charles Burnell

"J.R.'s lectures are a guide to being human and provide a map of the Maze in which we are often lost. They explain why we are the way we are, and how acupuncture can help transform and lead us out of the Maze."

—Danny Tapsell

"My acupuncturist recommended I study acupuncture and gave me Professor Worsley's book, *J.R. Worsley Talking About Acupuncture in New York*, to read. Before I reached halfway through the book, I was in love with acupuncture and in love with this inspirational teacher and I knew that I had to study acupuncture. I started school at the Worsley Institute in Miami Lakes in the fall of 1990 on a prayer and a shoestring budget and thanks to the love and generosity of the Worsley's, I am, fourteen years later, practicing acupuncture in Maryland and on the faculty of TAI in Maryland. This book can and will inspire many for many generations."

—Deanna Stennett

"I feel so blessed and honored to have had so much time to work with and be with J.R. Worsley. J.R. had such a great power to lighten and enlighten a human being."

—Patricia McNally-Gibbs